ST MARGARET'S WESTMINSTER

The Commons' Church within a Royal Peculiar

Also by Philip Holland:

The Governance of Quangos
Lobby Fodder?

ST MARGARET'S WESTMINSTER

The Commons' Church within a Royal Peculiar

Philip Holland

AIDAN ELLIS

To my wife, Jo,
for her never-failing support
and encouragement

First published in the United Kingdom by
Aidan Ellis Publishing, Cobb House, Nuffield
Henley on Thames, Oxon RG9 5RT

First edition 1993

A CIP catalogue record for this book is available
from the British Library

Filmset in Times by Contour Typesetters, Southall, Middx UB2 4BD
Printed in England by Biddles Ltd, Guildford, Surrey GU1 1DA

ISBN 0 85628 244 8

Acknowledgements

I am grateful to the Rector, Dr Donald Gray, for the help I have received from him. The book would not have been complete without his Preface.

I am very much indebted to the Abbey Assistant Librarian, Mrs Enid Nixon, not only for providing much of the essential research material, but also for her critical review of the draft manuscript and her subsequent advice. Mr Enoch Powell also submitted the draft to critical scrutiny, and as a result of these two reviews the text was greatly improved. Their specialist help was much appreciated.

I received valuable information in a report supplied to me by Mr Peter Foster, the architect in charge of the recent work of restoration. This provided answers to some of the questions raised by past historians as well as updating previous information about the structure of the church.

Detailed information about nineteenth century legislation was provided by Mrs P Burnett of the Oriel Room staff in the House of Commons Library, and I also benefitted from the researches of the

Secretary of St. Margaret's Belfry, Mr George Doughty. The photographs for the illustrations are the work of Mr Barclay Fleming, a member of the Abbey staff, to whom I am also indebted for advice on the selection of subjects.

Finally, my warmest thanks are due to the Dean, the Very Reverend Michael Mayne. He carries the major responsibility for the good family relationship that exists within the Abbey Close, and I am delighted that he has contributed the Foreword.

Philip Holland
January 1993

CONTENTS

Illustrations

photographs: courtesy Barclay Fleming

Foreword

I write this in my study, one of the few rooms in the medieval Deanery to survive the war. It is one of those rooms built about 1500 by almost the last, and perhaps the greatest Abbot to rule the Benedictine monastery of Westminister, John Islip. He oversaw the building of the Abbey's great Tudor Lady Chapel and the reconstruction of the chancel of St. Margaret's, which cost the then princely sum of £191. 11s. 1d. and which, in our day together with the rest of the church, has been most wonderfully restored.

This history of St. Margaret's comes as a celebratory postscript to this restoration, made possible by the successful £1 million Appeal launched by the former Speaker of the House of Commons, Lord Weatherill.

Many will be indebted to Sir Philip Holland for telling the story of a church whose history reflects that of our nation. No longer a parish church (yet widely known as 'The Parish Church of the House of Commons'), nor a Royal Peculiar (yet an integral part of the Royal Peculiar that is Westminister Abbey), St. Margaret's is uniquely itself. I welcome Sir Philip's initiative and commend his story of the church he knows intimately and greatly loves.

Michael Mayne
Dean of Westminster
January 1993

Preface

St. Margaret's? That's the small church next to Westminster Abbey, isn't it?, they say to me. Of course, as churches in central London go, it is a large church! It is only because it stands alongside the great bulk of the Abbey that it *looks* small.

But 'stand alongside the Abbey' is exactly what it does. This new history makes clear that St. Margaret's now has no independent existence apart from the Abbey. The whole of its maintenance and day-to-day financing is the responsibility of the Dean and Chapter of Westminster. My task as Rector is to be responsible to my capitular colleagues for this important part of our total witness, in the same way as they have their tasks as Canon Treasurer, Canon Steward, Lector Theologiae and so on. My appointment, like these others, is made or renewed annually by the Chapter.

In recent times there have been opportunities for the Chapter of Westminster to give careful consideration to the role of St. Margaret's, and certain things have become abundantly clear. One is that since the recent comprehensive refurbishment of the church, made possible by the enthusiasm of Speaker Weatherill in his Appeal, and brought about with great skill and sensitivity under the direction of our architect, Peter Foster, many have been reminded of the beauty and the potentiality of St. Margaret's as a fine place for Christian worship and celebration. Consequently, the Chapter has affirmed that this ought to be the church's primary function and purpose.

I would like to lay to rest a misconception about St. Margaret's. It is true (and very important to remember) that it is *not* a parish church; nevertheless, it is a very busy church. Although there is regular weekly worship only on a Sunday morning, each week sees a variety of other services and occasions. In this way, it is similar to its big sister and neighbour, the Abbey, but the services at St. Margaret's tend to have a particular 'slant'. Yes, not a parish church, but continuingly proud of its honorific title of being the Parish Church of the House of Commons. The provisions of the Westminster Abbey and Saint Margaret Act 1972 which protected the 'customary rights of the Members or officers of either House of Parliament in relation to Saint Margaret's Church or Westminster Abbey' are far from being a dead letter. Although there is no rule or regulation deriving from either church or state which invariably ties together the posts of Speaker's Chaplain and Rector of St. Margaret's, the fact that these offices have been continuously combined for the past twenty years has provided a welcome continuity in the Palace of Westminster.

Perhaps I can give you an indication of how this honorific role is actually worked out. At the time I write, what I have called the church's 'slant' becomes patently obvious. In the past seven days we have had a series of Services of Thanksgiving for the life and work of a wide range of people. First of all there was a service for a young government statistician, Andrew Darnbrough, whose life and promising career was cut short by cancer. The next service contained elements which made it a national occasion: a packed congregation celebrated the life of Baroness Ewart-Biggs. And a few days later a variety of ecclesiastical figures led the tributes and thanks to God for the life and far-reaching ministry of Bishop Oliver Tomkins.

Each of these three services was public and widely attended, but there was another, a couple of days ago, which was more private and understated. Each month, when Parliament is sitting, Members of Parliament of all political parties (and indeed, from different denominations) come together to celebrate the Holy Eucharist. After receiving Communion in St. Margaret's, they have breakfast together in Speaker's House and then listen to a short talk from a visting speaker. They then return to their responsibilities and burdens either as constituency Members or as Ministers of the Crown. For them, St. Margaret's serves as an oasis of devotion and contemplation within their hectic political lives.

There are a number of ways in which St. Margaret's has been affirmed as a place of united Parliamentary prayer. Just after the 1992 General Election, a large congregation attended a service for the opening of a new Parliament, at which the Archbishop of Canterbury preached. Joined by other church leaders, the Moderator of the General Assembly of the Church of Scotland led the prayers. Then again, each Advent, before they rise for the Christmas recess, the church is full to overflowing for the Parliamentary Carol Service, usually with lessons read by the Speaker and the Prime Minister. Thus we recall that when David Lloyd George, on 11 November 1918, and then Winston Churchill, on both 8 May and 15 August 1945, led the Commons across the road into St. Margaret's, these prime ministers were complying in their own day with an ancient tradition which is still far from dead at this present time.

A church then, as an eighteenth century writer put it, 'as it were, a national church, for the use of the House of Commons'. But it is a church which the Commons would wish to share with many, and so it is fitting that a former Member of Parliament should unfold, in detail, its history and significance to the interested reader. Such a history, as the Dean has said, touches the life and times of our nation at many fascinating and significant points and is well worth telling.

Donald Gray
January 1993

Canon of Westminster, Rector of St. Margaret's and Chaplain to the Speaker of the House of Commons

The Remembered Past

The exterior of St. Margaret's Church, clad as it is in Portland stone, gives no indication of the awe-inspiring beauty that greets the visitor entering by the great West Door and being confronted by the superb example of Renaissance glass in the East Window towering above the bas-relief copy of Titian's painting of *The Supper at Emmaus* behind the altar table. This coloured carving, which forms the centre-piece of the triptych below the East Window, was the work of Mr Seffrin Alken who carved it in lime-wood in the year 1753. The original painting by Titian was requested by King Ferdinand, King of Castile, Aragon, Sicily and Naples, at the beginning of the sixteenth century. Ferdinand is represented in the scene as the disciple on the left, and the second disciple is reputed to be a portrait of Cardinal Ximines. Charles V, the grandson of Ferdinand, is portrayed as the standing figure of the innkeeper wearing a Spanish hat, and the other standing figure in the background is said to represent either the future King Philip II or else a

1

Moorish slave in an allusion to the conquest of Grenada.

There was a long and widely-held view that the East Window was completed in 1504 to the order of King Ferdinand and Queen Isabella of Aragon and Castile, and was intended to be a gift for Henry VII on the marriage of their daughter Catherine to his son Prince Arthur. According to this view, the window was to be erected in the new Lady Chapel then under construction in Westminister Abbey. Completed after the death of Prince Arthur, so the story goes, it was rejected by his brother, Prince Henry, and given to Waltham Abbey. However, in 1867, Charles Winston suggested that the much more likely date for the manufacture of the window was about 1526. The two royal figures in the bottom left and right corners were not, as originally thought, Prince Arthur and Princess Catherine, but Henry VIII and his Queen Catherine.

W.R. Lethaby in *Westminster Abbey Re-Examined* (1925) and H. Read in *English Stained Glass* (1926) both consider that the window was probably made for the chapel of New Hall by a successor of Barnard Flower. There is some justification for the suggestion that the window was made for New Hall. The building had been acquired *c*.1517 by Henry VIII who subsequently spent several thousand pounds on its restoration and enlargement. If Winston's date for the manufacture of the window is correct, it is perhaps ironic that within months of this, Henry began openly to question the validity of his marriage to Catherine.

It is artistic merit that holds the attention of the visitor seeing the window for the first time. The design is typical of the Italian pictures of the period. The central light represents the Crucifixion with three angels holding chalices to receive the precious blood which flows from the Saviour's wounds. On either side of the cross are grouped masses of Roman soldiery, whilst at the foot are grouped the Virgin Mary, the Holy Women and St. John. Above the penitent thief an angel supports his soul in the guise of a new born babe. Above the unrepentant one hovers the Devil in the guise of a black monster dragging the thief to Hades. The upper lights show the crescent moon and the sun, and between them six angels hold the emblems of Our Lord's passion, the Cross, the Sponge on the Reed, the Crown of Thorns, the Hammer, the Spear, and the Nails.

As already recorded, the figures of Henry VIII and Queen Catherine occupy the bottom left hand and bottom right hand corners respectively. Above Queen Catherine, royally crowned, is her name-saint Catherine. Above the figure of King Henry on the left stands the Patron Saint of England, St. George, in full armour. Dr Farrar, who was Rector of St. Margaret's prior to 1895, when he became the Dean of Canterbury, described the East Window as 'a most precious relic', whilst Winston, the great Victorian authority on stained glass, cited the window in 1847 as the most beautiful work as regards harmonious arrangement of colouring with which he was acquainted.

Architecturally, the interior of the church offers a

fine and noble example of the English Gothic style of
the late fifteenth and early sixteenth centuries with
pointed arches, slim clustered pillars, and the vertical
lines of tracery of the Perpendicular period, most
marked in the East and West Windows. Following
earlier precedents, the 1991 work of refurbishing the
interior of the church included lime-washing the
stonework. Then twelve new electric chandeliers
were suspended from the arches on either side of the
nave. The effect has been to improve the quality of
the light in the church and to set in sharper relief the
beauty of the memorial windows, both old and new,
with which St. Margaret's is so well endowed.
Unhappily, enemy action during the Second World
War destroyed ten memorial windows and damaged
a number of others. One window over the East
Porch in memory of William Caxton was blown out
by bomb blast and only three small panels of the
stained glass were found to be intact. These were
fitted in the base of a plain glass window that had to
be erected in the North Aisle wall to replace the
irreparably damaged one in memory of Edward
Lloyd, Master Printer, who founded the *Lloyds
Weekly News* and the *Daily Chronicle* in the
nineteenth century. Thus the window serves not only
as a memorial to master printers, but like the war-
damaged Churchill Arch at the entrance to the
House of Commons, as a reminder of those who
continued to fulfil their responsibilities in the
building during the dark days of the war. The space
involuntarily vacated by the Caxton window over
the East Porch in 1940 was subsequently allocated to

4

a new memorial window dedicated in 1946 to Mr Speaker Fitzroy.

In the burial register of 1618 a single line records the name of Sir Walter Raleigh who was executed in Old Palace Yard, merely a few yards from the east wall of the church on 29 October of that year. His headless body was buried privately under the High Altar of St. Margaret's Church in Westminister. When Dr Farrar was the rector in the later years of the nineteenth century he drew the attention of an American friend, a Mr J.T. Lord, to the fact that Raleigh's body lay beneath the altar and that the only memorial to him was a brass plaque in the chancel. With the help of his fellow countrymen, Mr Lord raised the sum of £600 to pay for a large memorial window to replace the existing one over the West Door. The window is a striking page of history illustrated from an American point of view. The upper lights show angels holding two banners which contain respectively the Arms of the United States of America and the Royal Arms of the United Kingdom. Below are two shields to the left with the Arms of Edward the Confessor and those of the See of Westminster. Next to these are two angels holding the Tudor badge and the crowned harp emblem of Ireland. To the right of these are two shields bearing the Arms of the City of Westminster and those of the Abbey of Westminster. Below these, and in the centre, stands Queen Elizabeth the First. Next to her on the right is a portrait of Henry, Prince of Wales who was the son of James I and Raleigh's patron, and next to him is the portrait of Raleigh. The two figures on the left are the poet Edmund Spenser and the celebrated navigator Sir Humphrey Gilbert, who was Raleigh's half-brother. The panels below the portraits show Raleigh sailing for America and his landing in Virginia. They also show him presenting Edmund Spenser to Queen Elizabeth, his imprisonment, and his burial at St. Margaret's. A tradition peculiar to St. Margaret's which has been handed down from rector to rector asserts that Raleigh's severed head was buried in the same grave together with the body of his son, Carew Raleigh, in 1666. Near the East Porch a commemorative tablet to Raleigh ends with the words: 'Reader, should you reflect on his errors, remember his many virtues, and that he was mortal.'

The visitor facing west in the church will see to the right of the Raleigh window the memorial window to John Milton which had been presented to St. Margaret's in 1888 by another American citizen, Mr George W. Childs of Philadelphia in response to a letter from Dr Farrar. Mr Childs left the nature of the memorial to the discretion of his friend, the Rector, but asked only that the monument 'should appropriately commemorate the virtues and genius of Milton, whose works are held in as high esteem, and whose memory is as profoundly reverenced in this country, as in that of his birth.' The window was unveiled in February 1888 and among those present were Matthew Arnold, Robert Browning, Lewis Morris, the family of Mr Speaker of the House of Commons and the United States Minister and his wife. In the centre of the window is Milton dictating to his daughters *Paradise Lost*. Below is Milton as a boy at St. Paul's School, and Milton visiting Galilee. All around are scenes from *Paradise Lost*, with Satan awaking his legions, the Fall, and the expulsion from Eden. Above are four scenes from *Paradise Regained*. These show the Annunciation, the Nativity, the Baptism of Christ, and the Temptation in the Wilderness. At the top are jubilant angels and Adam and the Lord. In addition to the words of dedication, the window also includes four lines written by the American poet John Greenleaf Whittier:

The new world honours him whose lofty plea
For England's freedom made her own more sure
Whose song, immortal as its theme, shall be
Their common freehold while both worlds endure.

In the sermon preached by Dr Farrar after the unveiling of the window to Milton on the Second Sunday in Lent there occurred the following passage:
'To commemorate events of recent days the Members of the House of Commons, whose Church it is, have erected the window, which recalls the tragic death of Lord Frederick Cavendish; and memorials have been placed here to Lord Hatherley, the good Lord Chancellor; to Lord Farnborough who spent his life in the service of Parliament; and in token of our gratitude for fifty years of almost unbroken prosperity under the reign of a beloved Queen; the Caxton window was given by the Printers of London in memory of that great man who lies buried here; and Citizens of America, in their large-

handed generosity, and care for the great traditions which are their heritage no less than ours, have presented us with that brilliant West Window, which commemorates nothing less than the Founding of the New World.'

Balancing the Milton window on the other side of the West Door, the West Window of the South Aisle was erected at the turn of the nineteenth-twentieth century and is regarded as one of the finest specimens of stained glass of that period in the church. It is dedicated to Lord Frederick Charles Cavendish, son of the Duke of Devonshire, by his fellow Members of the House of Commons. He had been a Member of Parliament for seventeen years when, in the spring of 1882 he was appointed to the government as Chief Secretary to Ireland. In May 1882 on his arrival in Dublin, in company with and in the attempted defence of his associate Mr T.N. Burke, he was murdered in Phoenix Park. The upper lights of the window contain angels in various attitudes of devotion. The lower lights are divided into eight panels, four in each row, descriptive of the texts: 'He shall see of the travail of his soul, and be satisfied'; 'He is brought as a lamb to the slaughter'; 'He bearing His Cross went forth'; 'My flesh shall rest in hope'. The lower row panels are descriptive of: 'Thou hast been faithful over a few things'; 'Behold an Israelite indeed in whom there is no guile'; 'Behold I send ye forth'; and finally, 'Peace, be still'.

The windows of the North Aisle in addition to the damaged Caxton window, are, from the west, the W.H. Smith window, the Blake window, and the

Morris window. The window given by all-party Members of Parliament to express their respect for the Right Honourable W.H. Smith, MP who died in 1891 was unveiled on 15 March 1893. The window was described by Dean Farrar as having 'lustrous, almost jewelled glass, which is not merely painted, but the colours are actually burnt in; it is comparatively quite a recent invention, and this is the only window of the kind in the Church.' At the unveiling Dean Farrar's address contained these words: 'It might be said of Mr W.H. Smith, as was said of Archbishop Tait, that he never attempted less than his utmost, or did less than his best, and that he devoted the best efforts of his life to the service of his fellow men.' St. Margaret's parishioners at that time regarded the words to be equally applicable to Dean Farrar himself.

In the upper part of the window four angels holding scrolls reveal in order from the left 'B. 1825', 'W.H.', 'Smith', 'D. 1891'. The centre panel represents the Light of the World with a nimbus of glory round His head, His right hand raised to bless in the attitude of the Latin Benediction, His left hand holding the symbol of celestial wisdom, a lantern, and with emblems of darkness under His feet. To the right of the central figure is that of Cornelius the pious centurion clad in armour, but with sword, helmet and a roll of the law on the ground at his side, and with an angel hovering in the background. To the left Nathaniel is shown sitting beneath a fig tree reading the Scriptures with a dove at his feet in the background. The three pictures in the lower panel represent in the centre, Moses giving the Tablets of the Law to the Children of Israel; on the right, King David seated on his throne playing a harp; and on the left, Nehemiah superintending the building of the walls of Jerusalem.

The next complete memorial window is one erected by public subscription to honour one of England's greatest sailors, Admiral Blake, who had formerly been a successful colonel in the army of Oliver Cromwell. The upper lights show the letters 'R.B.' and four shields depicting in turn the Arms of the City of Taunton, and three coats of arms to which Admiral Blake had been entitled. The large lights in the centre of the window are portrayed as elaborate tabernacle niches. The centre panel shows Our Lord walking on the water and St. Peter sinking. On a scroll are the words, 'Lord, save me'. On the right is represented the Archangel St. Michael, the Patron Saint of the Church Militant and guardian of redeemed souls against his old adversary the Prince of Hell. He is fully armed and holds a shield charged with a cross, and with his cross-hilted sword he transfixes the old enemy the dragon at his feet. On the left is an angel called the Angel of the Sea, crowned with a rainbow and sandalled with flames. The lower lights depict Blake on the deck of his own man-of-war at Malaga; the Admiral's body being taken up the Thames from Greenwich for his state funeral at Westminister Abbey; and finally the reinterment of the coffin in St. Margaret's churchyard in September 1661.

Finally, in the north wall adjacent to the Chapel of

Christ the Intercessor, there is the window 'In affectionate memory of Edward Ashurst Morris who died 17 December 1890, aged 27. Erected by his brother, Alfred Morris'. The upper lights contain the monogram and coats of arms. The central lights are enclosed in elaborate tabernacle niches and represent the exquisite picture of the Nativity by Botticelli. In his *Life of Christ in Art*, Dean Farrar described the picture as one of supreme loveliness and full of divine meaning, adding that he had always regarded it as one of the sweetest and far-reaching sermons ever preached on the inmost meaning of Christmas Day. He went on to say '. . . it sets forth, above all, the doctrine of Savonarola, that the Incarnation meant "God and sinners reconciled" and "man made a little lower than the Angels crowned with glory and honour".' Below the scene of the Nativity the three lower panels depict in order from the left, the figure of Charity embracing little children, two brothers clasping hands, and a figure representing Fortitude holding a sword and buckler with a red cross. Mr Morris died only a few weeks after his first infant child had been baptized in St. Margaret's.

After the destruction of all the windows in the south wall they had to be temporarily filled with diamond panes of opaque 'bathroom' glass. In 1965, the War Damage Commission finally agreed to pay a sum of £3,700 in compensation provided it was spent on stained glass. With changing values this was just about enough to replace only one of the memorial windows destroyed. The Rector consulted

Mr John Piper, the artist responsible for the design of windows in Coventry Cathedral, the Roman Catholic Cathedral in Liverpool and Eton College Chapel. John Piper took the view that it would be unwise to have a single window of modern design in the south wall to compete with the glorious Renaissance glass at the east end of the church. He therefore suggested that if more money could be raised it might be possible to provide a complete glazing scheme for the whole of the South Aisle. This would not be with pictorial glass, but with carefully designed tinted, and delicately painted glass in a series of abstract patterns. The Rector agreed to launch an appeal for the extra funds needed and John Piper consulted Patrick Reyntiens who had always interpreted his designs for stained glass.

In John Piper's own words, he and Reyntiens 'decided to work with predominantly light coloured glass (green, grey-green, pale yellow, and near white). The aim was to provide an unaggressive screen or filter for the daylight on the south side of the church, which would be agreeable in itself and would in no way affect the grand vista eastward in the church.' In his letter of appeal for the additional £7,000 that would be needed to meet the cost of the whole scheme, the Rector, Canon Michael Stancliffe, had this to say: 'The design treats all the windows in the South Aisle as a unity, and fills them with pieces of glass of such quality, colour and size that the present lightness of the church will be increased rather than diminished. There will be no strong colours nor formal figures to distract the eye or compete with the great East Window. The artist's aim is to create a total impression of living radiance; shades of silvery grey will predominate, with pools and splashes of pale greens, yellows and blues in varied density. Those who have seen the full-scale cartoons are enthusiastic about the sunshine and liquid effect the glass will quietly produce even on the dullest days.' Inscriptions set in the wall below the windows perpetuate the names of those whom the original windows were erected in the late nineteenth century to commemorate. Below the second of the five full length windows in the South Aisle is the inscription: 'The windows in this South Wall designed by John Piper and executed by Patrick Reyntiens were dedicated by the Bishop of London on 15 January 1967 to replace those destroyed by enemy action between 1940 and 1942.'

Although only fragments of the Caxton memorial window survived the Second World War, a brass memorial tablet dedicated to him survived intact at the south eastern end of the church. His first shop was set up in the Abbey close by the Chapter House. From this shop in 1476 he produced his first book printed in England; it was Geoffrey Chaucer's *Canterbury Tales*. An active member of St. Margaret's, his name appeared in successive years on the church records assenting to the churchwardens' accounts. Like his father before him, he was buried in the churchyard, yet no memorial to him or his work had appeared in the Abbey or the church until the Roxburgh Club supplied the brass tablet to St. Margaret's in 1820. The tablet reads: 'To the Memory of WILLIAM CAXTON who first introduced into Great Britain the Art of Printing and who AD 1477, or earlier, exercised that Art in the Abbey of Westminster. This Tablet in remembrance of one to whom the Literature of this Country is so largely indebted was raised AD 1820 by the Roxburgh Club, Earl Spencer, K.G., President.'

It is not at all surprising that a church which has suffered more than most at the hands of the Puritans during the Commonwealth period, and from the effects of aerial bombing during the Second World War, should have lost so many of its older memorials, or that those which remain should not in all cases be continuing to occupy their original sites. Nevertheless, in addition to the profusion of wall plaques, particularly on the south wall, there still remain a number of more elaborate monuments worthy of attention. Among the older memorials still extant is a bust of Cornelius Vandun. He is remembered as a man who must have possessed the golden gift of silence to a remarkable extent since he had survived in office in the royal service through the four reigns of Henry VIII, Edward VI, Mary, and Elizabeth I. To keep one's head through such a period of service at such a tempestuous time in history was no mean feat. The inscription below his bust is as follows: 'Cornelius Vandun lieth here borne at Breda in Brabant a soldier with King Henry at Turney, yeamen of the gard and usher to K. Henry, K. Edward, Q. Mary and Q. Elizabeth, of hones and vertous lyfe, a careful man to poore folke, who at the ende of this towne did builyd for poor widowes

2 howses of his owne cost.' He died in 1577 from natural causes.

As St. Margaret's parish used to encompass the Royal Palace of Westminster, it is not altogether surprising that many members of the royal households worshipped there and, in due course, were buried there. Another such member was Blanche Parry whose memorial in the wall above her tomb shows her kneeling at prayer before a small altar table. The inscription below reads: 'Hereunder is entombed Blanche Parrye daughter of Henry Parry of New Courte in the County of Hereford. Esqier. Gentlewoman of Queene Elizabethes most honourable bedchamber and keeper of her Maties iuells whom she faithfullie served from her Highnes birth. Beneficiall to her kinsfolke and countrymen charitable to the poore insomuch that she gave to the poore of Bacton and Newton in Herfordshire seaven score bushells of wheate and rye yearlie for ever wt. divers somes of money to Westminster and other places for good uses. She died a maide in the eighte two yeers of her age the twelfe of February 1589.'

At the eastern end of the South Aisle there is a raised alabaster tomb with the recumbent figure of Lady Dudley who died in August, 1600. The inscription on the tomb also pays tribute to other members of her family who served their sovereign with great distinction. It reads: "Here lieth entombed Marie La: Dudley, daughter of Willi: Lo: Howarde of Effingham in his time Lo: high Admyrall of Englande, Lo: Chamberlayne, &: Lo: privy Seale. she was grandchilde to Thomas D: of Norff. the two of that surname: & sister to Charles Howarde, Earle of Nott: Lo: High Admyrall of England by whose prosperous direction thorough the goodne: of God, in defendinge his handmayde Q: Elizabeth the whole fleet of Spaine was defeated and discomfited.

'She was firste maried to Edw: Sutton, Lo: Dudley & after to Rich: Montpesson Esq: who in the memorie of her virtues, and last testimony of his love, erected this monument. She slept in Christ Jesus in the yere of our Lorde 1600 & the 21 of Aug: attending the joyfull day of her resurrection.'

Adjacent to the tomb is the stone figure of her second husband Richard Montpesson which had previously been attached to a nearby pillar.

To the left of Lady Dudley's tomb is that of the grandson of the Duke of Somerset who had been Lord Protector of England in the reign of Edward VI and who is not kindly remembered by St. Margaret's congregation for his attempt to destroy their church.

The tomb in which lie the bodies of Thomas Seymour and his wife Esable (Isabel) bears this inscription: 'Here in peace resteth ye bodyes of Thomas Seymour second sone to ye right honorable Edward Earle of Hartford & Esable his wife, eldest daughter to Edward Anley of Katesbye in ye county of Northampton Esq.: wch said Thomas departed this mortall life ye eight day of August 1600 & ye said Esable ye twentieth day of August 1619 in ye true faith of JESUS CHRIST and in ye blessed hope of a joyful resurrection.'

Another Elizabethan Lady of the Bedchamber has a monument above her tomb which is not dissimilar

in general design from that of Blanche Parry. It is
sited on the north side of the West Door and is in
memory of Lady Dorothy Stafford. It thus balances
Blanche Parry's monument in the wall on the south
side of the door. Like Blanche Parry, Lady Dorothy
is kneeling at a small table in prayer. It is however a
little more elaborate than the one on the south side
with a frieze below the main scene depicting three
men and three women at prayer, and an armorial
shield above the figure of Lady Stafford. Lady
Stafford had been married to Sir William Stafford,
but was widowed at the age of twenty-seven and
thereafter had served Her Majesty Queen Elizabeth
for a continuous period of forty years. Her husband's
grandfather had been the Duke of Buckingham and
her maternal grandfather was Lord Salisbury. On
her memorial plaque she is described by her son as
being '. . . loved by all, doing good to all she coulde
to every body, never hurted any, a continual
remembrencer of the sutes of the poore, as she lived
a religious life in great reputation of honor, and
vertue in ye world so she ended in continual fervent
meditation and harty prayer to God at ye wh instant
(as all her life) so after her death she gave liberally to
ye poore, and died aged of 78 years ye 22 of
September 1604 . . .' The place of her burial was in
accordance with her wishes.

On a brass plate on the south wall near the vestry
door are these words: 'I pray you remember Henry
Austen Layard, P.C., G.C.B., Discoverer of Nineveh.

'He served his Queen and his Country with all his
heart and with all his might while representing the

17

Boroughs of Aylesbury and Southwark in Parliament, as Under Secretary of State for Foreign Affairs, as First Commissioner of Works, as Minister at Madrid, and as Minister at Constantinople.

'Born 5 March, 1817. Died 5 July, 1894.'

Sadly one of the memorial windows destroyed by aerial bombardment in the South Aisle was the one given by his daughter in memory of Sir Goldsworthy Gurney who died on 28 February 1875 at the age of eighty-two years. However, the dedication remains on the wall below one of the Piper windows. Although his home was in Cornwall, he spent much of his time in the parish of St. Margaret's, mainly at the House of Commons. He originated the Electric Telegraph, High Speed Locomotion, and Flashing Light Signalling. He also invented the Steam Jet and the Oxhydrogen Blowpipe.

Ten years before the death of Lord Byron, his cousin Sir Peter Parker, Bt., R.N., the captain of HMS *Menelaus* was killed in America on 30 August 1814. At the time he was leading a commando raid up the Chesapeake to create a diversion in favour of the British army on the side of Baltimore. His late officers and crew donated a very handsome monument in his honour to St. Margaret's. It includes a bas relief likeness of Sir Peter and the scene of his death. Lord Byron composed a poem to his memory. The last four lines read:

> And, gallant Parker, thus enshrin'd,
> Thy life, thy fall, thy fame shall be,
> And early valour glowing find
> A model in thy memory.

Memorials to those who gave their lives in the service of their country are not uncommon in St. Margaret's, as indeed they are not in so many churches throughout the land. On the screen on the south side of the sanctuary there are two brass plates. One records the names of seven members of St. Margaret's choir who lost their lives in the armed forces during the 1914–18 war, and the other records the names of five members of the choir who died in the battles of the 1939–45 war.

Not all memorials are purely ornamental. Nor are they all necessarily 'designated' as memorials. One that qualifies, or risks disqualification, on both counts is the font that stands in the south-west corner of St. Margaret's. It is a fine example of the work of the celebrated English mason and architect, Nicholas Stone, who was responsible for carrying out the designs of Indigo Jones in the early seventeenth century and who completed the tombs of Bodley and Donne. The font was made in 1641 at a cost of ten pounds. It was originally ordered for a daughter church of St. Margaret's described by Stone as 'the new Chapell in Tutell filds'. As the chapel remained unconsecrated throughout the Commonwealth period, it is probable that the font was delivered direct to its purchasers, the church-wardens of St. Margaret's, and was set up in the mother church. The maker's own description of the font was as follows:

'A font of white Marble and Blake Marble . . . on the ground one great broad stone of 4 foote long, 3 foote and an halfe broad and 8 inches thick, wrought with a molding whereon is placed a basement of Blacke Marble and thereon a Pillar of white Marble wch doth support the bole of the Font being 20 ynches in diameter and 1 fotte thick of white Marble . . .'

The description is taken from Nicholas Stone's own notebook and was part of the estimate for the work. Although not so dedicated, the font is a worthy memorial to the skill and the work of Nicholas Stone.

Another memorial in regular use week by week, although in this case specifically dedicated to the father of the donor, is the Victorian pulpit. This was designed and donated by Sidney Vacher in the mid-nineteenth century in memory of his father Thomas Vacher, the parliamentary printer and publisher. In the year 1831, Thomas Vacher founded the Vacher's Parliamentary Companion which is still published quarterly to this day. On the flyleaf of each issue it used to be stated that it was intended to be an indispensible book for everyone concerned with parliamentary and national affairs. Many parliamentarians would agreed that it has fully achieved its objective.

Origin and Early History until 1540

The name of Saint Margaret, Virgin and Martyr, is recorded on 20 July in the calendar prefixed to the Book of Common Prayer. She was the Christian daughter of a pagan priest who lived in the third century AD in the small town of Antioch, now called Antakya in Turkey close to the border with Syria between Aleppo and the eastern Mediterranean sea. Olybius, the ruler of the territory and described by Mackenzie Walcott as the President of the East, tried without success to persuade her to marry him. Frustrated by her steadfast refusal, he took her prisoner and subjected her to physical torture to try to compel her to renounce her faith in Christ. When this failed to break her spirit or her faith, she was finally condemned to death in AD 292. As she faced the headsman's sword she bore witness to the simple truth that the strength of her Lord was made perfect in her woman's weakness.

In the eleventh century, Exeter Cathedral possessed among its relics the head of St. Margaret which apparently had been a gift from the Saxon King

Athelstan. Tradition has it that her body was embalmed and laid to rest at Monte Fiascone in Tuscany. She is one of the Guardian Saints of the Italian city of Cremona. In the sixteenth century, Marco Girolamo Vida, the Bishop of Alba from 1532 and known as the 'Christian Virgil', composed two hymns in her honour. She is usually depicted holding a book in her left hand and a cross in her right with which she pierces a dragon lying trampled beneath her feet. St. Margaret is depicted in this way on a large boss in the stone vaulting of the roof of the Chapel of St. Mary Undercroft beneath St. Stephen's Hall in the Palace of Westminister.

The first church dedicated to St. Margaret of Antioch in Westminister was built as a direct result of the decision of King Edward the Confessor to found a new Benedictine monastery on the site of the old Abbey church of St. Dunstan. Strong evidence supports the belief that work on the monastery was begun in the year 1051, the monastic domestic quarters were completed and occupied in 1061, and the Abbey church was consecrated in 1065, one week before the death of its royal founder. The Revd Mackenzie Walcott incorporated a precise date for the establishment of the parish church in the title of his book *The History of the Parish Church of Saint Margaret in Westminister; from its foundation, AD 1064*. This date had previously been given by the chronicler John Stow in his noted work the *Survey of London and Westminster 1598*. It is of course wholly feasible that, with the monks in residence and the Abbey church so near to its completion, the urgency of the need to establish a parish church to keep the laity out of the Abbey intended for the monks' exclusive use would have been clear in the second half of the eleventh century.

Gervase Rosser in his *Medieval Westminister, 1200–1500* states, 'St. Margaret's Church, possibly first built in the late eleventh century . . .', and support for Edward the Confessor's involvement is indicated in a document taken from the *Liber Niger Quaternus* which contains mainly fourteenth and fifteenth century items. Some time between 1474 and 1485 the document was made at the expense of Thomas Clifford who was a monk of Westminster from 1462 until 1485. The relevant part of the translation reads:

'OF THE PARISH CHURCH OF SAINT MARGARET
FIRST FOUNDED
BY SAINT EDWARD THE CONFESSOR

'A certain senior of this church (Westminster Abbey) a monk named John Tothale, who was present at, and assisted in, the coronation of King Edward the Third after the Conquest, was frequently wont to say that he himself saw a certain monk of the monastery who assumed the habit in the same place in the time of King Henry the Third. The latter was accustomed to relate that he heard his seniors asserting that in the time of St. Edward, who renovated this church anew from the foundations, the same Saint of God for the greater honour and peace as well as of the monks as of the parishioners founded the first church of St. Margaret in the place where it is now situated . . .'

From the beginning, the sole responsibility under the Pope for St. Margaret's Church and parish was the jealously guarded prerogative of the Abbot of Westminister. Within that framework the local inhabitants in their role as parishioners evolved their own means of communal association and activity. In the year 1189 on St. Margaret's Day, 20 July, the Abbot and Convent of Westminster procured a Papal Bull from Pope Clement the Third. This confirmed that the church of St. Margaret was outside the jurisdiction of the Bishop of London. This confirmation became necessary because the authority of Westminister had been challenged by Gilbert Folliot, Bishop of London from 1161 until 1176. It was again challenged during the Primacy of Archbishop Stephen Langton who, sitting with other papal judges in 1222, gave judgment in favour of Westminster against the Bishop of London and the Chapter of St. Paul's recognising the exempt status of the Abbey and the parish church. St. Margaret's was thus declared to be wholly exempt from any authority after Rome, except that of the Abbot of Westminister; and so it remained throughout the later Middle Ages.

From the beginning, St. Margaret's enjoyed considerable prestige not only arising from its royal patronage, but also because of its geographical situation in the town of Westminster. Westminster's importance grew from its position on the Island of Brambles, more commonly remembered by its

Anglo-Saxon name of Thornea. The suffix *ea* in Saxon means an island. This was an island in the Thames. Fords connecting Thornea to the north and south banks of the Thames at that point provided a link between Watling Street and the Dover Road. Westminster thus became an appropriate place for a half-way house where the Yorkshire woollen merchants met the Flemish weavers to transact their business. With the development of the wool trade between England and the Low Countries, Westminster grew as a commercial centre and as a focal point for our international trade. Not entirely surprisingly it became a magnet for the nation's rulers, and the obvious choice for the seat of government. In 1353 the establishment of the Wool Staple set the seal of success on the commercial activities of the town.

The first church dedicated to St. Margaret survived as an eleventh century Romanesque structure without a tower until the reign of Edward III. Then, in the latter part of the fourteenth century, the parishioners and very many wool merchants rebuilt almost the whole church from its foundations, replacing the old nave with a Perpendicular one. Only the great chancel was untouched, since this had been well maintained in good repair by the Abbot and Convent of Westminster acting in their role as Rector. By this time, St. Margaret's was not the only place of parochial worship within the area. Before the end of the twelfth century, consent had been obtained from the Abbot and Convent to build a chapel on their estate in Westminster for the use of the church of Exeter and all future bishops of that See. As a condition, provision was made against any possible prejudice or loss to the church of St. Margaret which might result from the new building. Much closer to the Abbey and St. Margaret's was the church of St. Mary Magdalene in the area of what is now Tothill Street. There were also the chapels of St. Ann in the Almonry, of St. Armille, of Our Lady of the Well, and the Collegiate Chapel of St. Stephen which was situated within the precincts of the neighbouring Royal Palace of Westminster.

Nevertheless, the parish of St. Margaret's covered a total area of forty-four square miles north of the River Thames. Its boundaries on a modern map of London would be shown by a straight line from Lambeth Bridge to the eastern end of the Serpentine in Hyde Park, a curve which followed the northern curve of the water to the Bayswater Road, and then a straight line to the junction of Oxford Street and Holborn. From there the boundary line would be round to the Thames, taking in Soho Square, Long Acre and Covent Garden. However, the priests responsible for St. Margaret's services continued to remain under the the direction of the Abbey until as recently as 1841 when the Rectory was separated from the Abbey.

This subservience to the Abbey of St. Margaret's priests was underlined during the turbulent reign of Richard II late in the fourteenth century. During that period the Abbot directed his monks to refrain from distant pilgrimages and ridings abroad in order that they should make a solemn procession every fourth day around the Abbey boundaries, and on every sixth day through the whole town of West-minister. In these processions every chaplain and clerk within the parish of St. Margaret was ordered by the Abbey to take part.

Thanks to a vast collection of records preserved in the Westminster Library, including a remarkably complete set of St. Margaret's churchwardens' accounts from the year 1460 onwards, there is a wealth of historical detail available about the church and those who served it from the middle of the fifteenth century. The earliest set of accounts relates to the years 1460 and 1461. They were written entirely in Latin until 1467. During the next seven years both Latin and English were used in their compilation and then from 1474 they were written entirely in English.

During this period there was a small vicarage next to the south wall near to the west end of the church. As an annex to the vicarage, with direct access to the church, there was a small apartment measuring fifteen and a half feet by nineteen and a half feet. This was designed to provide accomodation for an anchorite. A number of items in the churchwardens' accounts refer to sums paid to the 'anchorite in residence' for tending the church and other menial tasks such as laundering church garments. The anchorite's vow of solitude was not only the pre-rogative of men. In fact the early churchwardens' accounts show that the occupant of the anchorite cell attached to St. Margaret's was more commonly a woman. Although they were highly esteemed, they were not overpaid for the valuable work they performed. In 1469, for example, we learn from the accounts that four pence was paid to St. Margaret's hermit for watching and making clean the church.

The earliest surviving accounts are not of course only historical records of expenditure. The sources of revenue also bring to light more than a hint of manners and customs long since fallen into disrepute. From the earliest accounts of the middle-to-late fifteenth century it appears that one of the principal sources of income was the money collected on the various 'gadering', or gathering, days. In the earliest records, these days were Pentecost, St. Margaret's Day, All Hallows Day, the Nativity of our Lord God, Good Friday, and Easter Day. The collection at Easter was set aside for the cost of the Paschal Candle. It is also interesting to note that in the year 1488 the word Pentecost was replaced in the accounts with the word Whitsonday. The 'gatherings' or collections took place sometimes in the church, sometimes at the church door and sometimes from house to house.

At about this time the Good Friday gatherings were stopped and replaced by collections made on 'Hock Monday' and 'Hock Tuesday'. The earliest known use of the word 'hock' occurred in the year 1250 in the rule of the Abbey of Shrewsbury. Its meaning is lost in obscurity but Hock Monday and Hock Tuesday were the components of a two-day festival kept in the third week after Easter. This was entirely secular in character both in its origin and its observance. On the Monday the men would set out with cords to bind those of the other sex whom they met. They would then keep them captive until the women bought their freedom with a small sum of money. On the Tuesday, the men would be held hostage by the women and in turn would have to buy their freedom.

Towards the end of the fifteenth century St. Margaret's, not for the first time, had fallen into such a desperate state of delapidation as to be in need of almost total reconstruction. A start on this mammoth task was made thanks to the generosity of Lady Mary Billing, the widow of Sir Thomas Billing, the Lord Chief Justice of England. At entirely her own expense she provided all the funds necessary for the rebuilding of the South Aisle of the church. This was sometimes called the Trinity Aisle, taking the name from the 'Trinity Altar' which stood at the eastern end of the aisle near the entrance to the present vestry. Mary Billing died in the year 1500 before the completion of the rebuilding work, but her example of pious munificence provided a great stimulus for the parishioners, already envious of the grandeur of the Abbey, to find the means to continue the good work. A stone in her memory is in the South Aisle.

In 1491, Henry VII made a grant of land to facilitate the extension of St. Maragaret's, but before commencing the work of new construction to take advantage of this, the parishioners applied their efforts to the decoration and furnishing of the new South Aisle, and the vestry attached to it. The walls were painted and additional expense was incurred in fitting out the vestry. A chest containing vestments for the priests of St. Margaret's which had been kept in the Abbey vestry was sent for, as was another chest of church plate. Both chests were then installed in the new vestry. Two great new candlesticks were provided by funds received from the sale of old brass, and various other payments were made for essentials not included in the financial provision made by Lady Mary Billing. According to the copies of the accounts these included the sum of four pounds for covering the new aisle with a lead roof.

The churchwardens' accounts of 1497 show that payments were made for repairs to the west end of the church. For the next three years this work was carried on in an intermittent way to avoid as much disruption as possible, with the continuance of corporate worship. The roof was first made secure and weatherproof before the slow replacement of the walls, section by section, was begun. From 1499 onwards, however, the accounts show the purchase of building materials to have been made regularly and continously over a number of years. These purchases included thirty tons of Caen stone in 1499, and large quantities of stone, lead and timber in the following years. Meanwhile, the furnishing of the church was being largely paid for by private benefaction and general expenditure from the churchwardens' account. One of the gifts was a pair of coral beads embellished with silver and gilt, and a little ring set with a pearl stud given 'to the worship of God and Our Lady and St. Margaret to be hanged upon the image of St. Margaret every day or else every holy day'.

The accounts first make reference to 'masters of the tower' in those dated 1498–99 and it was therefore almost certain that this would be the date when building began on the present tower. By 1515 the work was completed on the tower and for the next eight years the churchwardens were chiefly concerned with meeting the cost of materials and labour for the steeple which was completed in 1523. The work on the main body of the church had continued until 1515. Whilst other work was in progress, Abbot Islip took the opportunity to replace the obsolete Romanesque chancel and to transform the church into the fashionable form of a 'hall church' with no structural break between chancel and nave. The number of masons employed on the church work varied from time to time. In 1500, for example, the number of masons varied from three to five and their wages fluctuated between three and four shillings a week. No account of the work would be complete, however, without some mention of the pious generosity of the workmen themselves. The master mason, Mr Redman, returned his wages in full as regularly as he received them, and smaller financial gifts were also regularly contributed by the other masons, the chalk men, the smith, the plumber and the carpenter. St. Margaret's has always been greatly loved by those who serve it.

By 1523 the newly completed church was deemed to be in a fit state for 'hallowing' although it was still in debt for some of the work done. To meet the running costs of the work of reconstruction, the churchwardens decided that they would be justified in pledging the church plate. Some of it went to several of the fraternities connected with the church as security for loans. Other items went to secure loans from individuals. For example, in 1519 one of the churchwardens advanced a sum of sixty-eight pounds and received in return 'the best crosse of silver all gilt', two chalices, two silver bells and various other articles. At the end of 1520 the debt amounted to £139.

However, before the hallowing of the church took place on 9 April 1523, sufficient money had been borrowed to redeem the various items of plate that had been lent as security. Most of the new loans came from five of the fraternities connected with the church, namely the Fraternity of St. Cornelius, the Brotherhood of St. Anne, Our Great Lady Brotherhood, the Fraternity of Our Lady of Rouncyvall, and the Brotherhood of St. Christopher.

It was not unusual in the late Middle Ages to pair St. Margaret with St. Catherine who, in effigy, was distinguishable by her torture wheel. So, after the completion of the rebuilding of the church a Roger Weston of St. Albans was commissioned to make two wooden tabernacles in honour of the two saints. These were large decorated frames constructed to contain the statues of St. Margaret and St. Catherine which had previously stood together in the chancel. St. Margaret's tabernacle incorporated three stories of St. Margaret carved in relief which, like twelve additional small images on the same tabernacle, were painted and gilded. The tabernacle of St. Margaret was erected over the north side of the High Altar in 1525, and that of St. Catherine over the south side of the altar two years later. Above each tabernacle was suspended a martyr's crown. For making the two tabernacles Roger Weston received the sum of sixty pounds in three instalments. Raising the money to pay for these elaborate furnishings typically involved the whole parish. The gilding of St. Margaret's tabernacle was more than paid for by the generosity of the Virgin Mary's guild as well as sixty donors from the parish. Three of the fraternities made additional contributions totalling eight pounds, whilst the collection taken at the May Day festivities brought in a further sum of thirty-four shillings and ten pence. Another seventy individual parishioners contributed ten pounds expressly to meet some of the cost of St. Catherine's tabernacle. Throughout its history this has always been a well-loved church, and appeals for help have invariably been met with a ready and generous response from all sections of the public.

The interior of this renovated and refurbished church of St. Margaret must have been strikingly beautiful. There was the rood with attendant figures of the Virgin Mary and St. John before which a lamp burned continously. There was the High Altar with richly gilded tabernacles and the two side altars of Our Lady and the Trinity with many other altars in the aisles. There were brightly hued statues contrasting with the more subdued colours of the stained glass of the period. The whole, encased in richly

33

carved stone and timber, must have lived long in the memory of all who were privileged to see it.

Until 1534 the churchwardens' accounts record regular annual expenditure on the promotion of a festival of feasting, music, dancing and drama to celebrate St. Margaret's Day. The celebration took place not late in July, near to the actual date, but on the first Sunday in October which was designated as St. Margaret's Dedication Day. Habitually the day began with a parochial feast at which the 'worshipful of the parish' were entertained with 'bread, ale, wine, and other things'. Special cloths were borrowed from the Abbey and elsewhere to hang in the church. Garlands of red roses decorated the chapel and image of St. Margaret, and faggots were purchased to make a bonfire on the eve of her festival. A regular feature of the day's proceedings was a procession through the town of the virgins of Westminster led by minstrels. Along the route of the procession a collection was made from the passers-by towards the maintenance of the church. In 1518 the accounts show an entry of the receipt of eight pence from the children of the May-game, which could have been a performance of a flower-decked 'maypole' dance or a set performance in the nature of Maid Marian and Robin Hood.

The payments recorded for St. Margaret's Day in 1522 include eight pence paid to Mistress Ford in reward for the virgins' clothes, and twelve pence paid for a minstrel to play for the virgins. The accounts for 1485 list a substantial number of items of expenditure for St. Margaret's Day when clearly a special effort was made in what proved to be a year of great historical importance. For this occasion eight pence was paid to two watchmen to be on duty on St. Margaret's night. Twelve pence was paid for bread, ale and wine for the singers of King's Chapel. The cost of hiring, hanging up and taking down banners of silk and gold in the church totalled three shillings and six pence.

Two years later a boat had to be hired to go from Westminster to Sheen to fetch rich hangings to decorate the church, and then to return them to Sheen afterwards at a total cost of four shillings. Seven years later the cost of putting on a play on St. Margaret's Day was eight shillings whilst the charge for the ministrels who led the procession of virgins was seven pence. Two minstrels were employed in that year.

For preparing the accounts for 1529 and 1530, the Curate, Sir Henry Mote, received a payment of thirty shillings from the churchwardens' account. He left before the accounts were approved and this was done by his successor, Master William Tenant. However, Henry Mote seems to have returned later as his name reappears several times in the accounts dated from 1540 onwards. He also appeared in the accounts dated between 1524 and 1528. The first time was the occasion when the churchwardens set up a new tabernacle in the church and spent five shillings and four pence on a new surplice for Master Mote, the Curate. This was presented to him on the very clear understanding that if he went out of the parish he would leave the surplice behind him. The second entry relating to Henry Mote shows that he was one of the eighty subscribers to the cost of the new tabernacle.

The surplice lasted for nearly ten years before it apparently became necessary for the churchwardens to replace it for another curate in 1534 at a cost of ten shillings. In the same accounts, surplices for the two clerks and the sexton cost three shillings each. These last surplices contrast with the price of four surplices for adults purchased in 1523 at a price of eight pence each.

Although St. Margaret's was substantially restored and refurbished in the eighteenth, nineteenth and twentieth centuries, the chancel, the nave, the aisles and the tower are essentially those of the church hallowed on 9 April 1523. The splendid Perpendicular interior with its superb slender pillars, and the very fine tracery of the East and West Windows bear ample testimony to that. The present East Window brought to Westminster at Parliament's expense during the restoration of 1758 was manufactured in Holland early in the sixteenth century at about the same time that the church was undergoing its major reconstruction in that period.

Early in the sixteenth century the outside of the church was beautifully proportioned and elaborately decorated. Soon the effect of this was totally marred by the press of houses being built on sites in St. Margaret's churchyard and close to the Abbey. A row of nine or ten houses occupied the ground immediately to the east of the church and were actually joined to the church wall. On at least two occasions permission was given to the occupants of these houses to make windows into the church through their common walls to enable them to attend the services without leaving their homes. A survey of the north wall of the church for the restoration work to be carried out in the late twentieth century revealed that this had also probably been a partition wall between the church and a row of dwellings. Indeed, leases for tenements in the churchyard were granted with such frequency during this early part of the sixteenth century that they covered much of the ground close to St. Margaret's and the Abbey. Not only did this proliferation of buildings obscure the beauty of church and Abbey alike, but they constituted a serious fire hazard to both. Nevertheless, it was not until the early years of the nineteenth century that the demolition of the houses enabled St. Margaret's to occupy the open and conspicuous position that it has at the present time.

The ten years from 1530 to 1540 were singularly uneventful in the life of St. Margaret's, unless the ending of the virgins' procession through the town on the day dedicated to St. Margaret could be called an event. In the world outside St. Margaret's however, the progress of the Reformation was gathering pace, and pressure was increasing on the monastery and Abbey church dedicated to St. Peter. On 30 March 1533, Thomas Cranmer was duly consecrated as Archbishop of Canterbury. As a portent of things to come he took the oath of allegiance to the Pope coupled with a protest that he took it 'for form's sake'. Then in 1534, under the aegis of Thomas Cromwell, both Houses of Parliament passed the Act of Supremacy. This was followed during the last four years of the decade by the dissolution of the monasteries. The first monasteries to go were the smaller ones, and then a second Act was passed to abolish the larger ones.

So it was that on 16 January 1540 the monastery at Westminster was surrendered to the Crown. On that day the rectorial rights over St. Margaret's previously exercised by the Abbey were consquently in abeyance. On the same day, the churchwardens of St. Margaret's acting with commendable speed, briefed a learned man, Mr Chidley, to draw up a Bill 'to the King's Highness for the Churchyard and to his Clerk for ingrosynge the same'.

The cost of this service to the churchwardens' fund was six shillings and two pence. It was money well spent for it achieved its objective. Thirty weeks later the churchyard passed into the hands of the churchwardens of St. Margaret's and for the first time payments for the graves in the churchyard were paid to them instead of to the Abbey. This continued for two and a half years until the patent of endowment of the new foundation made it possible for the former Abbot, now installed as the new Dean of the Abbey church to reclaim the rectorial fees.

Tudors and Stuarts from 1540

T he upheaval in religious houses throughout the land caused by the break with Rome was not immediately discernible to the visitor to St. Margaret's. The rood-loft still stood, the lamp continued to burn in the sanctuary, the richly ornamented Tabernacle of St. Margaret which had cost three pounds to have gilded in 1531 held pride of place by the High Altar, and the Trinity Chapel remained enriched by the presence of the Tabernacle of Our Lady of Rouncyvall for which secure iron clamps were purchased and fitted more than a year after the Abbey had been surrendered to Henry VIII by Abbot William Boston. However, some changes were made that were indicative of the larger changes taking place elsewhere. The heading on the church-wardens' accounts was amended to include the description of Henry VIII as 'and on earth Supreme Head of the Church of England and Ireland'.

In those accounts there also appears an item of the payment of ten pounds to a glazier, Symon Symons, for 'making and setting up divers arms in the Trinity

Chapel . . . by the advice and commandment of Mr Lancaster Herrolt-at-Arms'. Those arms were in fact the Arms of the King, Prince Edward, and the Lord Privy Seal. Another item in the same accounts reports the payment of one shilling and four pence for four loads of sand spread in the churchyard when the King attended Mass. Probably as a result of the King's visit, the churchwardens were put under some pressure to make more substantial changes. However the time lapse between the King's visit and the next phase of acquiescence in change indicates some reluctance, even resistance, to change by St. Margaret's. It was not until 1545 that a table was purchased for the High Altar and a lectern made for the Bible. In the same year six books of the Litany in English were bought.

In 1546, the accounts record the sale of the Tabernacle of Our Lady of Rouncyvall which had been set up in the Trinity Chapel only five years earlier. The Tabernacle of St. Catherine which had also stood in the Trinity Chapel was sold in the same year. Early in the following year two more tabernacles which had stood by the High Altar were sold for forty shillings. Later in the same year of 1547 the churchwardens' accounts reveal that three shillings was paid to 'the poore men that did bear the Copes and other necessaries to knightsbridge when that King Henry the Eight was brought to his burial at Winsor and to the man that did ring the bells'. They also show that eight pence was paid to the 'Ringers at King Henry the Eight his dirge in the Parish Church'.

The work of divesting the church of all signs and symbols of Roman Catholicism did not stop with the death of Henry VIII but continued throughout the six and a half years of the reign of Edward VI. The records show that during those years not only were items of furniture such as tabernacles and altars removed and when possible sold either complete or piecemeal, but the disposals also included richly ornamented vestments and even the linen squares previously used in the Catholic Mass. During the earlier years of the reign of Edward VI, when his uncle the Duke of Somerset was Protector, the church itself was threatened with destruction.

Somerset decided to build a magnificent palace for himself. He fixed on a site in the Strand at that time occupied by the old church of St. Mary and the episcopal palaces of Worcester, Lichfield and Llandaff. The material provided by their demolition, however, proved to be insufficient for his needs so he decided to take down St. Margaret's and have provision made for the St. Margaret's parishioners to worship in a part of the nave of Westminster Abbey. No sooner had the workmen arrived with their scaffolding, however, than a huge crowd of parishioners armed with bows and arrows, staves, clubs and other offensive weapons gathered around the church. This so terrified the workmen that they ran away and flatly refused to return to carry out the work. So the resolution of those who loved St. Margaret's triumphed.

The destruction and disposal of many of the church's treasures, however, was finally stopped only after the death of Edward VI in 1553 when the staunchly Roman Catholic Mary Tudor succeeded him. Shortly afterwards Sir Thomas Wyatt, with the father of Lady Jane Grey, led a rebellious army of Kentish men to Southwark. In an unsuccessful attempt to capture Ludgate, he and a number of his followers were taken prisoner and executed. Three of his adherents who had been executed were buried in St. Margaret's churchyard on 8 February 1554: they were Anthony Adamson, Edmond Perry and John Sympson. The final curtain on the rebellion came down when St. Margaret's bells pealed out on Ash Wednesday in celebration of the victory and overthrow of Wyatt.

More violence occurred at St. Margaret's on Easter Sunday in 1555. William Flower, otherwise known as William Branch, attended Mass at St. Margaret's. He afterwards claimed that he had been compelled to do so by the Spirit. At the solemn moment of the administration of the Sacraments, he attacked the officiating priest with a sword so that 'the chalice with the consecrated hosts, being in his hand, were sprinkled with his blood'. He was immediately seized and committed to the gatehouse prison. On the following Friday he was cross-examined about his views on the Sacrament. He replied, 'Do what ye will, I am at a point; for the Heavens shall as soon fall, as I will forsake mine opinion' and a great deal more besides. He was sentenced to death and burnt outside St. Margaret's churchyard five days later.

Following such an outrage within its walls there

had to be a formal 'reconciliation' of the church. This duly took place according to the Roman Catholic procedure, and the bishops taking part in the ceremony were subsequently entertained at the expense of the churchwardens. The accounts relating to this shed light not only on the price of food in 1555, but also on the level of hospitality which custom demanded on these occasions. Food provided at the dinner included three capons at a cost of seven shillings, half a calf for five shillings and six pence, four geese for two shillings and four pence, a dozen rabbits for two shillings and eight pence, a dozen pigeons for two shillings and six pence, and a sirloin of beef at a cost of six shillings and eight pence. The bishops' dinner was washed down with two gallons of wine bought for two shillings. The lesser mortals were entertained in the vestry with bread, beer and ale for a total cost of three shillings and two pence, the bishops' servants received a cash sum of ten shillings and the bell-ringers on that occasion were paid the sum of eight pence.

By this time, the churchwardens had been busy purchasing new materials and items for use in the Catholic Mass, and engaging the necessary workmen to repair and refurbish the church. In the course of the past two years they had had to spend about ninety pounds in undoing the work of the previous ten years. Their purchases included a Mass book, two grails, a blue satin chasuble, a canopy for the Sacrament, a fringe of silk for the canopy, a copper censer, a copper and gilt cross, a taffeta cloth with a picture of the Holy Trinity for the cross, and a lantern to be borne before the cross at the Festival of the Visitation. Ten shillings and eight pence was paid for repairs to two copes, two vestments, one hearse cloth, and for the alterations necessary to convert a cope into a chasuble. A further fifteen pence was paid for making two albs.

In spite of Queen Mary's ruthless campaign against Protestants, life at St. Margaret's appears to have stayed on an even keel during the final years of her reign. The last two years saw the restoration of the celebration of St. Margaret's Day and the revival of such festive customs as the use of holly and ivy to decorate the church at Christmas. Seventeen candlesticks were obtained for the rood-light, and a mason, Nycholas Clarke, was paid forty shillings to take down an old figure and convert it into an image of St. Margaret. For those two years the fullest splendour of equipment and furniture was retained in the church. Mary Tudor died in November 1558 and bonfires of celebration were lit in London to mark her passing and the end of persecution.

On the accession of Queen Elizabeth the bells of St. Margaret's rang and the choir sang a *Te Deum*. In due course Queen Elizabeth attended a Mass at the church. Shortly afterwards, recognising that it would be politically advantageous for her role in Europe to be that of a Protestant sovereign, she issued a proclamation to the effect that the church service be read in English and the elevation of the Host be discontinued. Pope Paul IV responded with a declaration that since Elizabeth Tudor was illegitimate, she must surrender all claims to the crown.

He went on to assert that, as England was a fief of the Holy See, only he had the right to decide who should ascend to the throne. The result of this was to make Protestantism and patriotism synonymous in England. The effect of this on St. Margaret's during the second and third years of Elizabeth's reign was to create a revival of destruction which left the church, if anything, barer than before.

The churchwardens' accounts for 1559 show that payments were made for the removal of the table at the High Altar and the holy water container. They also record payments for the removal, cleavage and sawing of the rood which bore the images of St. Mary and St. John. The 1560 accounts offer a long list of items in metal, timber, and cloth sold to various merchants. For example, the heavy beam on which the rood-loft was supported, together with boards and other timber salvaged from the destruction of the rood-loft were sold to Andrew Holbourne for forty-two shillings. A chandler of London, Robert Wallters paid eighteen shillings for a pound of old wax, and a further twenty-three shillings for a quantity of brass and brass alloy. Two years later a certain John Royall was paid six shillings for his work in dismantling the St. George's loft. From 1570 onwards the records show the progressive removal of much that remained to make the church beautiful, apart from its architecture and its structural stonework.

For the most part, during the reign of Queen Elizabeth the history of the church itself is uneventful by comparison with the earlier years. However, the history of Elizabethan England is well recorded in the parochial documents. All the Queen's travels to and from Whitehall, Greenwich and Hampton Court were marked by the bells of St. Margaret's, as were all the principal events of her reign. They rang again in February 1587 to mark the execution of Mary, Queen of Scots. Mary Stuart, having been forced to abdicate by the Scots in 1567 sought the protection of Queen Elizabeth in 1568. During the nineteen years of her detention in England, a large Catholic minority looked to her as the likely restorer of the old faith. She was naturally a constant source of anxiety to the Queen and her advisers, but it was not until Sir Francis Walsingham produced some evidence of her approval for the Babington Plot to assassinate Elizabeth and place herself on the throne of England that Mary was condemned to death and executed on 8 February 1587.

In 1588 when news of the approach of the Spanish Armada reached England, Queen Elizabeth went to Tilbury to address her assembled army. Again the bells of St. Margaret's rang out, as they did shortly afterwards on her return to London. During these years there appear many items in the churchwardens' accounts of payments to glaziers. These indicate the replacement of plain glass windows with more colourful stained glass ones. At the same time other payments are shown for the whitewashing and adornment of the pillars and for a painter's work on the pulpit and font. Thus it would appear that Queen Elizabeth's brand of Protestantism was not as austere as that of Calvin or even that of Edward VI.

Beauty and colour were being restored to the interior of St. Margaret's.

Although 1665 stays in the mind as the year of the great plague in London which decimated the population, the story of that onset of bubonic plague began during the last three decades of the sixteenth century. In no fewer than forty-nine of the years between 1570 and 1666 references to the plague appear in the records. It was thought that infection was spread by dogs and cats. Thus entries in the church accounts showing payments made to the 'dog killer' were not uncommon throughout the period. For example, in 1592 there were three such payments made. The first was a payment of sixteen shillings made to the dog killer for killing dogs at the first sign of infection. The second was a further payment of ten shillings and ten pence for killing more dogs. The third item was a payment of seventeen shillings and sixpence made to the 'poor men for the killings of dogs'. In 1603 the burial register for St. Margaret's shows the deaths of more than nine hundred to whose names the plague mark is attached. In later years the number for St. Margaret's parish alone grew to more than 1,500 in a twelve-month period.

During the later years of the reign of Queen Elizabeth, St. Margaret's was subjected to no further visible alterations to its general appearance or furnishings. There was, however, a considerable hardening of opinion in favour of the new Puritanism which became increasingly apparent in St. Margaret's rigid adherence to the letter of the Book of Common

47

Prayer and other Puritan practices such as the use of common bread in the Holy Eucharist. Many bishops, who in the reign of Queen Mary had sought refuge in Switzerland, returned after her death influenced by the doctrines of Calvin. Their return naturally had an effect on the thinking of many churchmen in this country. Thus it was that the form of service in St. Margaret's tended to differ in certain particulars from the more ceremonial procedures followed in the Abbey services. It was due to these differences that on Palm Sunday, 17 April 1614, a new special relationship between St. Margaret's and the House of Commons was born. It has already endured for nearly 400 years, although from time to time the framework within which it continues has been slightly modified to accord with the changing times.

On that Palm Sunday the House of Commons for the first time ever attended in its official capacity the service of Holy Communion at St. Margaret's on the occasion of the opening of a new Parliament. Prior to this, the practice had been for the Commons to join with the House of Lords to attend parliamentary services in the Abbey on such occasions. When for reasons of their own, the Commons decided not to accompany the House of Lords to the Abbey, they would remain in their debating chamber, St. Stephen's Hall in the Palace of Westminster, until the monarch and the members of the Lords arrived at the Palace for the State opening. The Commons would then be summoned to attend the sovereign and their Lordships in the Upper House.

In a debate in the House of Commons on 13 April

1614 a complaint was made that the Abbey did not administer the Communion with common bread and that such omission was contrary to both the twentieth Canon and the Book of Common Prayer. A motion was made therefore by Sir James Perrott and Master Fuller that the whole House should receive Holy Communion together on the following Sunday, but not at the Abbey church as originally planned. Instead, the Commons would attend St. Margaret's Church. The original proposal for the Commons to participate in a corporate Communion came from the member for Haverford West, Sir James Perrott, on 9 April. He had strong Puritan sympathies and equally strong anti-Spanish prejudices but was one of the most popular and experienced debaters in the House of Commons with an attractive personality. Supervisors were appointed to check on the attendance and participation of all members, and Mr Speaker was instructed to appoint a preacher for the occasion. There is no record of the name of the preacher but it is known that neither he nor the officiating ministers would accept any remuneration for their services. Mr Speaker and a committee of four other members were therefore appointed to administer the distribution of the collection taken.

During this period the appointment of a curate in charge of St. Margaret's rested with the Dean and Chapter as Rector. He was invariably a minister with duties at the Abbey as well. However, as curate of St. Margaret's he was required to preach on the first Sunday in every month and four times during the year additionally. As the church services obviously required more than this a lecturer was appointed as an assistant. The lecturer, like other parochial officials was selected, and owed his appointment to the Vestry. Not all who preached in St. Margaret's therefore were chosen to do so by the Dean and Chapter of the Abbey in their role as Rector. However, when again in January 1621 the Commons decided to attend another corporate Communion in St. Margaret's and on that occasion selected Dr Ussher to be the preacher, the Dean and Chapter strongly objected on the grounds that since St. Margaret's was within their jurisdiction, the House of Commons had no right to nominate a preacher. In the words recorded by John Pym, MP, 'This put the House into some heate, and thereupon it was resolved to change the place of the Communion from Westminster to the Temple.'

The Temple Church in the Inns of Court was an obvious alternative since this was a stronghold of the legal fraternity which was, as always, strongly represented in the House. On second thoughts, however, the House decided to appeal to James 1. He supported the Commons against the ruling of the Dean, but advised Dr James Ussher privately 'that he had charge of an unruly flock to look to next Sunday.' So the Commons had its way and Dr Ussher duly preached at St. Margaret's on Sunday 18 February 1621.

In 1624 the churchwardens of St. Margaret's built a school for poor children in the parish. Since the school uniform was green, the school became known as the Green Coat School to distinguish it from the Brown Coat School established in Westminster in 1601. The Brown Coat School had been endowed by Lady Dacre, a parishioner of St. Margaret's and a Maid of Honour to Queen Elizabeth, 'for the comfort and entertainment of certain of the honest and aged poor of the City of Westminster . . . and also for the instruction of certain of the boys and girls of the said City in the knowledge of the Christian religion and such other learning as may fit them to earn their livings in soberness and industry'.

Apart from its common usage today, the word 'hospital' also has the definition of 'a charitable institution for the education of the young'. So the Charter of Incorporation granted by Charles 1 in 1633 to the Green Coat School included these words: 'Whereas divers of our loving subjects dwelling within our City of Westminster have resolved to settle a certain House, in which boys and girls of tender years may not only carefully be maintained with meat, drink and apparel, but also be instructed in manual arts, in a certain part of a farm of the Dean and Chapter of St. Peter's, Westminster, and have humbly supplicated us, so much as in us, to found and erect that House into an Hospital . . . Know ye that we being willing to further their pious intentions . . . do will and ordain that the House be an Hospital, and that the same hereafter be called by the name of the Hospital of St. Margaret's in the City of Westminster, in the County of Middlesex, of the Foundation of King Charles . . .'

The hospital was subsequently referred to in

official documents as 'the Hospital of Greene Coat Boyes in Tothull Fields in this Parish'. The school relied almost entirely on charitable bequests and donations mainly from active supporters of the work of and at St. Margaret's. Not all the income received was, however, donated in the name of charity. The accounts of St. Margaret's churchwardens dated 1628 show an item which reads, 'Received of divers persons the parishioners of this parish, for their fines for swearing and being drunk, and for the breach of the Sabaoth, and being otherwise accountable to the penal laws, as by a particular of their names and several fines appeareth, which hath been employed for the use of the hospital children, the some of £3. 9s. 4d'.

Two further hospitals with facilities for teaching the young were established in Westminster in 1654 and in 1674. The first, which became known as the Black Coat School for obvious reasons, was thanks to the generosity of the Revd James Palmer, who had been born in St. Margaret's parish and later became Vicar of St. Bride's Church in Fleet Street. The second was the work of a great local benefactor and churchwarden of St. Margaret's who had previously contributed to the founding of St. Margaret's hospital school. His name was Emery Hill. Eventually in 1873, Queen Victoria approved the amalgamation of the Green Coat School with the schools of Emanuel Hospital, Palmer's Hospital and Emery Hill's Hospital to create what is known today as Westminster City School. The Foundation Board in the School Hall commemorates the four benfactors of the foundations after which the school houses are named.

During the Civil War, in 1644, half-way between the drawn battle of Edgehill and the Parliamentarian victory at Naseby, but with Cromwell controlling London, a renewed campaign of church despoilation was taking place. In St. Margaret's Church 134 pounds weight of brass was removed from various tombstones and sold for three pence a pound, whilst a further twenty-nine pounds of fine brass from the more expensive tombs was sold for four pence a pound. In the same year the screen and organ-loft were torn down and sold for five pounds whilst the organ pipes fetched a further four pounds.

Indeed, St. Margaret's, the Parish Church of the House of Commons, was one or the first to suffer from the power given by the House in 1643 to a committee of nine of its members to 'demolish the same where any superstitious or idolatrous Monuments are informed to be: And all Churchwardens, and other Officers, are hereby required to be aiding and assisting in the Execution of this Order'. As early as April 1643, a royalist newspaper published in Oxford carried a report that 'a Committee thereto authorized by the House of Commons and guarded by a band of soldiers, purged St. Margaret's church in Westminster of all the scandalous pictures (that is to say all painted glasse) in the windows, and of the statue or images in the tombs and monuments'.

On Monday 25 September 1643 there occurred an historic occasion of special significance in the annals of the Commons' Church, when the Solemn League and Covenant was ratified within its walls by both Houses of Parliament, the Westminster Assembly of Divines, and the Scottish Commissioners. In the months that followed the signing of the Covenant, the sermons at St. Margaret's attracted unpredecented congregations. So much so that in November 1644 the House of Commons was obliged to order that the gallery of St. Margaret's should be reserved for the sole use of Members of both Houses of Parliament on every Day of Humiliation or Thanksgiving. The intensity of revolutionary dogmas invariably varies throughout the course of the revolution. So it was at St. Margaret's. In December 1648, in an extremist Puritan sermon from the pulpit by Hugh Peter in which he denounced Charles Stuart as 'the great Barabbas, murderer, tyrant, traitor' one month before the same King Charles Stuart was tried and executed in the parish of St. Margaret's, it may be said that Anglican fortunes in England reached their lowest ebb. Yet by 1653, St. Margaret's was reported to be again 'keeping the Holy Dayes with joy and alacrity, not without hope of good times to succeed'. The church was also reported to have restored and refurbished the font previously banished to the churchyard at the command of the Commons.

One of the first acts of St. Margaret's Vestry to mark the end of the Commonwealth and the return of King Charles II was to pass a resolution authorising the restoration of the Royal Arms in the church. According to the resolution, these were to be 'verie richly carved and gilded with all the grace and comeliness that may bee and after the best manner that can be invented, and that they may be as faire rich and beautiful in everie respect as the Kings Armes are sett up in any Church within or about the Citie of London'. St. Margaret's did not, and does not believe in half measures.

By an Act of Parliament in 1660 the clergy who had been turned out of their livings by force during the Cromwellian period, were restored to their parishes in their hundreds. The result of course was to impoverish the many clergy who had been appointed to those parishes during the Commonwealth. St. Margaret's, ever mindful of its need to show Christian charity irrespective of the rights or wrongs of particular cases, gave financial assistance to five dispossessed priests living in the parish and charged the sum to the parochial account. The enormous increase in poverty in the 1660s, engendered largely by the climacteric year of the bubonic plague and the Great Fire of 1666, was a major problem that seriously engaged the attention of the church officials. To help the parish to cope with the problem, a request was made to the Dean and Chapter that any money arising from the profits of the market, or collected in the Abbey for the poor, might be handed over to St. Margaret's churchwardens for immediate distribution. The request was granted and the Dean also promised to give thirty pounds a year out of his own pocket so long as the special needs continued to exist.

In the late 1660s difficulties arose over the seating arrangements in the church. As a result strict regulations had to be made and enforced to prevent dissension growing among the parishioners. No persons were to be seated in either of the front pews in the middle ranges of the gallery unless they were either present or past burgesses of the parish, whilst the second pews in the same ranges were to be reserved for those who were or had been their assistants. When a pew was definitely let, it was the duty of the churchwardens to conduct the tenants to the pew, see them take their places, and deliver to them the key of the pew door. It was further ordered that neither the gallery keeper, nor any person acting for him, should presume to open the door of any pews in the gallery to allow them to be occupied by people other than the tenants without the prior permission of the tenants themselves. The gallery keeper was also forbidden to accept any quarterly payment from anyone not a seat holder on pain of penalty or dismissal.

Other matters claiming the attention of the church officials arose from complaints about early morning and late evening ringing of the bells. By ancient custom a bell was rung at five o'clock in the morning and at eight o'clock in the evening. The addition of three bells between 1650 and 1680 to make a ring of eight had stimulated the bell-ringers' activities much to the annoyance of the local people. The problem was resolved by the introduction of a rule prohibiting the ringing of bells, at least in peal, before seven in the morning or after nine at night. Six years earlier, the Vestry had been obliged to introduce more stringent regulations with regard to the belfry. In

1674 a boy of fourteen had been drawn up by one of the bells and killed. The subsequent enquiry showed that the keeper of the bells had been very slack in the performance of his duties. Instead of being constantly in the belfry to supervise the ringers, he had left a number of boys there and absented himself for no good official reason. As other misdemeanours were also proved against him, he was dismissed.

The installation of a new organ in 1675 was the occasion for Dr Outram, the Curate, to effect a change in the conduct of services, introducing a higher musical content. The Vestry then appealed to Dr Outram to restore the former practice and asked that 'the Clerk may read every verse of the singing psalms' as had been done before the installation of the organ.

For a number of years at this time, the question of repairs had been requiring continual attention. Work was first begun on restoring the chancel, the tower, the west end of the church, and the windows. When this work had been satisfactorily completed the advice of Sir Christopher Wren, the architect of the new St. Paul's Cathedral, was sought on the question of a new gallery to be erected over the South Aisle of the Church to match the one over the North Aisle. After lengthy, and at times acrimonious, debate the decision was taken to go ahead and the arrangements were left in the hands of Sir Christopher. The new south gallery was finally completed and brought into use for 'persons of quality only'. The pulpit was then ordered to be transferred into the middle of the body of the church where it effectively denied most of the congregation any view of the altar.

As a consequence of these alterations, some considerable changes had to be effected in relation to the siting and assignment of the pews. After lengthy arguments it was finally decided that the front six pews should be allocated to certain leading parishioners at rents varying between twenty pounds and six pounds, but with the added condition that the pew holders should be responsible for lining their pews with green 'in a uniform manner as the churchwardens still direct'. The whole cost of the gallery over the South Aisle was met by Sir John Cutler, knight and baronet. The cost of moving and erecting the pulpit on its new site was met by another parishioner, Mr Hugh Squire. The new organ by Bernard Smith cost £200 of which nearly £175 was contributed by certain anonymous 'persons of quality' in the parish. After the completion of these internal changes, the year 1682 saw, for the first time, the assignment of a particular pew for the specific use of the Speaker of the House of Commons. He was to have the 'Westmost of the two high pews in the middle row'. The eastmost of the two high pews was divided to provide accommodation in the one part for the reader and in the other for the clerk.

Eighteenth and Nineteenth Centuries

The joint coronation of William III and Mary II brought to an end the period of extreme religious and political changes that had scarred the sixteenth and seventeenth centuries. However, the parish of St. Margaret's celebrated that event in 1689 in much the same way as it had celebrated the coronation of Charles II following the demise of the Commonwealth. The parish met the cost of providing a hogshead of claret, 'music and all such things as have been accustomed on such occasions'. The new monarchs' arms were set up in the former East Window which was described by an early eighteenth century writer as containing 'several Figures within Mascles (diamond shapes) painted on the glass but without proper design for the place'.

The opening years of the eighteenth century were years of controversy, jealousies among church dignitaries, and disagreements within the Church. St. Margaret's was not immune from this general malaise. In 1713, the appointment of a new Dean of Westminster, Francis Atterbury, did not exactly improve relations between St. Margaret's Vestry and the Abbey. In the same year a vacancy occurred at St. Margaret's for a parish clerk. Trouble arose from the announcement that the Dean would be responsible for making the appointment. It was contained in a Chapter minute of July 1713 and read as follows: 'The place of Parish Clerk of St. Margaret's being now vacant, and the Dean and Chapter as Parson of the said church having an undoubted right to dispose of that Place, They do agree that when a Fit Person is nominated thereto by the Dean, they will defend the Right of the Church of Westminster in that behalf.'

After taking conflicting advice from four eminent counsel, the Vestry sent the following reply to the Dean: 'Resolved that this Vestry does not acquiesce in the Dean of Westminster's appointment of Roger Gethin to be Clerk of this Parish'. The reply was dated 28 July 1713.

The Vestry thereupon appointed a former organist to fill the vacancy. Two days later the Dean visited the Vestry and asked to see the old records. This was refused. Following further acrimonious exchanges one of the churchwardens was ordered to appear before the Ecclesiastical Court of the Dean and Chapter and instructed to hand over the vestry books under pain of contempt. The Vestry again refused, counsel were briefed and the matter was eventually resolved in its favour. However disputes between church and Abbey continued for the next nine years. Dean Atterbury had already established a reputation for arousing dissension in his various church appointments and his career came to an end in 1722 when he overstepped the mark by becoming involved with the Old Pretender in an invasion plan. As a consequence he was removed to the Tower of London, though continuing in office as Dean until 1723.

On 22 January 1722 a petition was presented to the House of Commons signed by the current minister of St. Margaret's and the two church-wardens, Robert Kidwell and Matthias Sayer, on behalf of themselves and the parish residents. The petition drew to the attention of the House that despite the considerable sums spent each year on building maintenance, the church and tower were nevertheless deteriorating into a condition of serious delapidation. As a result of the anxieties of those who came to worship each Sunday the church structure and tower had been surveyed; and the survey indicated that the necessary repairs would cost at least £3,000. The petitioners then requested that the necessary money for the repairs might be forthcoming from the revenue obtained from a duty already being levied on coal. This special tax had been imposed by Parliament to finance the building of fifty new churches in the cities of London and Westminster. It was pointed out in the petition that much of this specific levy was being borne by the inhabitants of the parish of St. Margaret's. Nevertheless, the House of Commons turned down the petition.

By 1734, the minister and churchwardens had learned some of the lessons of their earlier failure to prise support from the Commons and so they presented a new petition couched in rather different terms. It was recorded in the House of Commons Journals in the following way:

'A petition of the Minister, Churchwardens, Vestrymen, and others of the Parish of St. Margaret, Westminster, on behalf of themselves and the rest of the Parishioners, being offered to be presented to the House. Mr Chancellor of the Exchequer, by His Majesty's command, acquainted the House that His Majesty, being informed of the contents of the said petition, recommends it to their consideration; that the said petition was brought up and read, alleging that the expense of making commodious, beautifying, and repairing the Church of the said Parish, which this House and their predecessors have made choice of to honour with their presence, having their particular appointment of seats therein, to attend Divine Service, together with the purchase, repairs, and furniture of a workhouse, has created so great a parish debt, yet remaining unsatisfied, and occasioned such heavy annual rates, to which a much smaller number of inhabitants are now subject . . . therefore, and in regard to the circumstances of the said Parish, and their having formerly received favours from an House of Commons to repair their Church, praying the House to grant them such assistance as will enable them to make repairs suitable to the Church which has the honour to receive the Representatives of the People of Great Britain, the expense whereof by computation will amount to about £3,500.'

That extract from the Journals of the House of Commons was dated 28 February 1734. The Journal dated 18 March 1734 contained the following note: 'Resolved that a sum not exceeding £3,500 be granted to His Majesty for the repair of the tower and roof of the Parish Church of St. Margaret, Westminster.'

As a result of this it was possible for repairs to be carried out to the walls and roof of the church and for the tower to be largely rebuilt and cased. In 1737, the House made a further grant of £1,590. 18s. 5d. towards the cost of further restoration and refurbishing work and this was followed two years later by another payment of £2,000. Clearly the 1734 reminder of the privileges enjoyed by members of the Commons at St. Margaret's, and the special relationship existing between House and church, had touched at least a few hearts and loosened a few purse strings.

In 1753 the coloured triptych behind the altar table was carvd in lime-wood by Mr Seffrin Alken. The centre panel depicts the Supper at Emmaus and is a copy of the painting of that name by Titian completed some 200 years earlier. The reredos does not follow the more customary practice in churches throughout the land of depicting the Last Supper and this has a message for all who worship in St. Margaret's. It is a message of joy as it depicts a moment of supreme happiness in the history of Christianity, when the two disciples first came to the joyous realisation that the Stranger who had joined them on the road to Emmaus was in fact their Risen Lord.

Five years later the House of Commons voted a further sum for St. Margaret's of £4,000 'for the purposes of new pewing and decorating the Church'. As has happened both before and since that date, with a little help from other benefactors, the sum was enlarged to include not only the purposes specified by the main donor, but also to build a vault throughout the whole length of the church, as well as ornamenting with new gilding the above ground interior of the church. The vault, which still exists though it is now sealed, is subdivided into a number of separate chambers. It is to these chambers that the remains of some of those who had previously been buried in St. Margaret's churchyard were transferred when it was decided to terminate the use of the churchyard as a burial ground. It is reasonable to assume, therefore, that many of those former residents of Westminster whose names live on in the history of our island kingdom have thus found their last resting place beneath the floor of the nave and chancel of the church.

Parliament made a further grant in 1758 of £400 specifically to make it possible for the church-wardens of St. Margaret's to purchase the magnificent East Window. During the 230 years of its existence it is reputed to have had a number of owners following its original acquisition by Henry VIII. These are believed to have included Sir Thomas Boleyn, the Earl of Essex, the Duke of Buckingham and General Monk, before eventually being sold to a Mr John Conyers of Copt Hall, Essex for fifty guineas. His son later sold it to the churchwardens of St. Margaret's for 400 guineas. In spite of its travels before reaching its final resting place above the altar, it remains a very fine example of Renaissance stained glass.

In 1761, two more bells were added to the belfry to make St. Margaret's one of the first churches in the country to have a ring of ten. A Vestry minute of 1763 records a resolution that the figures of St. Peter and St. Paul should be painted in imitation of statutory by Mr Casali, and placed in the niches on each side of the altar of the church. Two Parliamentary grants of £6,721 in 1799 and of £4,500 in 1802 enabled further work to be carried out. A new pulpit and reading pews were erected in 1803, and the Speaker's Chair was placed in front of the West Gallery. In July 1804 most of the houses which had filled the space on the north side of Henry VII's Chapel in the Abbey were demolished and preparations were well advanced to enclose the building with an iron railing similar to the one enclosing the north side of the nave of the Abbey. The House of Commons was moved to make a further grant of £3,059 in 1813 to help meet some of the costs of the extensive internal alterations that were taking place. How extensive these were was indicated in a report dated 1824.

The Christening Pew, formerly situated in the ambulatory at the eastern end of the church was then converted into a room and, with a partition which had hitherto divided it from the church removed, it was made accessible to the congregation. The font had been sited near the pew under a Gothic arched ceiling, and enclosed with railings. The entrance to the vault was also enclosed to correspond with the Christening Pew and the ends of the galleries were enclosed by Gothic glazed screens. Where the pews had previously been covered in green baize, they were now lined with drab coloured cloth. A new entrance to the church was made at the east end and the entrance on the south wall was closed. The West Window was glazed and iron drain-pipes were laid round the south and west sides of the church. The pulpit which had hitherto obstructed the congregation's view of the east end of the church was moved to its present site, and finally a large bronzed warm-air stove was placed in the middle of the nave. Lest it should be thought that the House of Commons was the sole support of church maintenance at this time, it should be mentioned that the parishioners contributed some £15,000 in the same period for the work of repair and refurbishment.

Something of the breadth of the church's ministry may be judged from the terms of the obituary notice of Dr Fynes Clinton, Prebendary of Westminster and Curate of St. Margaret's, which appeared in the *Gentleman's Magazine* for December 1827. 'The most useful characters in the sphere of ordinary life are not those which form the usual subjects of panegyric. The continued and gentle operation of a well spent life is unobserved and unostentatious. Such was the tenor of the life of the departed. In it, however, the charity and goodwill of that religion, of which he was a minister, were not to be mistaken. The poor of Westminster will remember the hand that liberally ministered to their wants; and the love of peace and harmony, which guided his actions and threw their grace upon his demeanour, will not soon be forgotten.'

In 1834 the Houses of Parliament, with the exception of Westminster Hall, were burnt to the ground due to a faulty heating system. Thanks to the heroism and energetic efforts by Mr Black, the Assistant Keeper at the Rolls Court, the ancient records of Parliament were rescued and placed within St. Margaret's Church for safe keeping until more permanent and secure accommodation for them could be arranged.

As St. Margaret's was conveniently close to the House of Lords, and most bishops of the day were able to maintain London establishments, it was by no means unusual for ordinations to be held in the church. Among those ordained there in 1883 was Robert Gray who became the first Bishop of Cape Town. Another ordinand, eight years later, was Dr John Mason Neale, the hymn writer and founder of St. Margaret's Sisterhood in East Grinstead.

From its foundation in 1604, St. Margaret's had been subordinate to the Abbey to the extent that first the Abbot and later the Dean and Chapter had been *ex officio* the Rector of St. Margaret's. The priest in day-to-day charge was designated variously as chaplain, minister or curate and was appointed by the 'rector'. Junior priests known as lecturers were appointed and paid by the parishioners themselves. However, as the population of Westminster grew it became apparent that St. Margaret's was not sufficiently well organised to be the parish church for such a large and growing town. So in 1840 the link between the church and the Dean and Chapter was severed largely due to the initiative of the Tory reformer Sir Robert Peel. He included in an Act of Parliament the provisions that St. Margaret's should become part of the Diocese of London and that one of the canons of the Abbey should be appointed by the Crown primarily in order to be a parish priest as rector of St. Margaret's. Henry Hart Milman, M.A., who had been the Curate of St. Margaret's and Prebendary of Westminster from 1835, was appointed to be the first independent Rector in 1840 and remained in the post until he became Dean of St. Pauls in 1849.

Reference has been made to the use of St. Margaret's for ordinations, and these continued under the new regime. The last occasion on which a bishop officiated at an ordination in an episcopal wig was in 1848. This took place at St. Margaret's and the officiating bishop was Doctor J.H. Monk, the Bishop of Gloucester and Bristol.

On 21 March 1855 the House of Commons attended a special 'Fast Day' service in honour of those fighting in the Crimea. The preacher on that occasion, Henry Melvill, failed to strike the right note for the assembled congregation. Comment on this is available in a contemporary note written by a newly elected MP, Stafford Northcote. He described how he went to St. Margaret's 'with the House – that is to say, about 150 members and the Speaker. Oddly enough I was placed next to Disraeli, who entered into conversation with me very amicably afterwards, and agreed with me that the sermon was exceedingly "flash". Every now and then the preacher paused at the end of a flowery sentence, and the whole congregation coughed and sneezed approvingly, exactly as if they were cheering. I was a good deal disgusted.' The following year on 4 May the House again adjourned to St. Margaret's for a service of general thanksgiving for the signing of the peace with Russia. This was altogether a happier occasion and there seem to have been no recorded complaints about the preacher on that occasion.

The next time that the House of Commons attended St. Margaret's as a corporate body on a state occasion was on Sunday, 22 May 1887. Their purpose was to offer thanksgiving on the jubilee of the reign of Queen Victoria. As this was an event which had never previously occurred it was felt that it demanded and should receive a stately if simple ceremonial response. The fact that Archdeacon Farrar was then the Rector of St. Margaret's was of itself a guarantee that the opportunity would be exploited to the full. A report of the event published in 1888 in *Queen Victoria: Her Life and Jubilee* gives a very clear picture of what happened: 'Members met in their places in the House before eleven o'clock in the morning, and the arrival of the Speaker at the Clerks' table signified the time for attending the service.

'Just before the clock struck a quarter to eleven the Speaker, Mr Peel, arose and walked down the Chamber to the door, the Members forming behind

him in order, four abreast . . . altogether about four
hundred . . .

'On the procession passing out of Palace Yard
into Parliament Square, it was joined by the band of
the Queen's Westminster Volunteers, who, playing
an appropriate march, led the way with slow and
measured pace, as befitted the dignity and character
of the participants and the function. It was nearly
five minutes after the hour appointed for the com-
mencement of the service when the West door of St.
Margaret's was reached and the procession entered
the Church, their progress having been awaited by a
great crowd of six or seven thousand well dressed
persons . . . The scene in the Church was exceedingly
animated, though, of course, it was marked by a
fitting solemnity and quietude of demeanour. The
seats in the nave were reserved for Members, those in
the two aisles being set apart for their ladies . . .
Meanwhile the Archbishops of Canterbury and
York had taken their places on either side of the altar
table, which was slightly decorated with flowers,
while in front of it stood some splendid specimens of
the azalea in full bloom.

'. . . The Speaker, who wore his full bottomed wig,
and his state robes richly embroidered with gold,
took his seat in the front pew with his predecessors,
Viscounts Eversley and Hampden. Mr Erskine, the
Serjeant-at-Arms, who had borne the Mace thus far,
placed it on rests constructed specially for the
purpose in front of the Speaker . . . The service
opened with the singing of the National Anthem;
and, as the choirs of Westminster Abbey and St.

Margaret's were combined for the occasion, and the congregation joined heartily in the singing, the effect was very grand. Archdeacon Farrar read the second lesson from Romans xiii, the first (1 Kings iii 5–14) having been read by the Honourable and Reverend T. Byng, the Speaker's Chaplain. The Absolution was pronounced by the Archbishop of York and the benediction at the close of the service by the Archbishop of Canterbury. After the third collect Handel's well-known Coronation Anthem was sung with much effect, and then followed a fine hymn composed expressly for Her Majesty's Jubilee by the Bishop of Ripon, and set to music by Dr Bridge, who had introduced into the tune the melody known as 'Gotha' composed by Prince Albert. This hymn of praise and worship was entitled 'For the Priceless Gifts' and at its conclusion the sermon was preached by its author, the Bishop of Ripon, whose discourse, remarkable for its power, brilliant illustration, and sustained eloquence, was listened to with intense interest.

'. . . During the singing of the final hymn a collection was made on behalf of the funds of Westminster Hospital. . . . The amount collected was one hundred and eighty seven pounds. The service closed with the Hallelujah Chorus . . .'

The last time that the House of Commons had the occasion to thank a preacher in its traditional form was ten years later in respect of the sermon preached by Dr Farrar in St. Margaret's on Sunday, 10 June 1897 'at their Public Thanksgiving for the completion of the sixtieth year of the reign of Her Majesty,

71

Queen Victoria'. Dr Frederic William Farrar, English clergyman and writer of considerable repute, had been ordained at the age of twenty-three in 1854. He taught at Harrow and then became headmaster of Marlborough in 1871. In 1876 he vacated his appointment at Marlborough to become a Canon of Westminster and the Rector of St. Margaret's. Whilst continuing as the Rector of St. Margaret's – to which he had been appointed by Benjamin Disraeli – he was also appointed to be Archdeacon of Westminster in 1883 and Chaplain to the Speaker of the House of Commons in 1890.

Dr Farrar was widely recognised as a superb preacher, parish priest and author. During the time that he was St. Margaret's Rector he worked ceaselessly to have the church repaired, improved and refurnished. The restoration work he set in train was the last such work to be supervised by Sir Gilbert Scott. He was the author of many ecclesiastical works but is perhaps best remembered as an author for his two Victorian best sellers entitled *The Life of Christ*, and a school story, *Eric, or Little by Little*. While Rector of St. Margaret's, his sermons attracted so many people to come and hear them that his congregations were frequently larger than the ones attending either the Abbey or St. Paul's Cathedral. The West Porch of St. Margaret's which was designed by J.L. Pearson contains a memorial to his work. In 1895, Dr Farrar became the Dean of Canterbury and it was in this appointment two years later that he was invited by the House of Commons to preach at St. Margaret's on this auspicious occasion of thanksgiving.

As the traditional thanks to Dr Farrar from the House of Commons appeared as the last entry of its kind in the Commons Journals it should perhaps be quoted in full.

Friday, 2nd July 1897

Commemoration Service in St. Margaret's Church

RESOLVED, *Nemine Contradicente.*

THAT the Thanks of this House be given to the Very Reverend FREDERIC WILLIAM FARRAR, D.D., Dean of Canterbury, for the Sermon preached by him on Sunday the 20th day of June last before this House in St Margaret's Church, Westminster, and that he be desired to print the same; and that Mr Balfour and Secretary Sir Matthew White Ridley do acquaint him therewith.

REGINALD F.D. PALGRAVE
Cl. Dom. Com.

During the last fifteen years that he was Rector of St. Margaret's the church was further embellished by the addition of a quantity of richly-coloured Victorian stained glass in no fewer than eleven memorial windows. These included the Queen Victoria Jubilee window, and the windows in memory of Lord Hatherley, Lord Farnborough, and Edward Lloyd who founded the *Daily Chronicle.*

Unhappily none of these windows survived man's inhumanity to man in the Second World War. Of the other seven windows erected between 1880 and 1895, the Caxton window was partially destroyed and the unscathed panels that did survive have been inserted in the plain glass window which replaced the original Edward Lloyd window. The six survivors from that period are the memorials to Sir Walter Raleigh, Admiral Blake, W.H. Smith, Lord Frederick Cavendish, Edward Ashurst Morris and John Milton. Before the end of the century, Dean Farrar had also been responsible for erecting a memorial window in the inner vestry to his son Cyril Lytton Farrar who was born at Harrow on 18 March 1869 and died in Peking on 2 February 1891.

St. Margaret's has for long been noted for the high quality of its music, and the foundation for its present standard of excellence was undoubtedly laid in 1897 by the installation of the organ built by Walkers. It continues to the present day to be regarded by the experts as one of the noblest parish church organs in England. Meanwhile St. Margaret's hospital centres of learning had grown in the late nineteenth century from 307 pupils to 850 pupils in 1888. In 1890, therefore, it was decided to rename the group Westminster City School. Over the years the school has been an excellent source of supply of choristers for St. Margaret's and thus played a notable role in helping to maintain its musical reputation.

Dean Farrar was succeeded as Rector of St. Margaret's in 1895 by the Revd Robert Eyton, M.A.

who administered to the needs of the church and parish for the next four years. The Rector during the year 1899 only was Dr Joseph Armitage Robinson who then became first the Dean of Westminster and then the Dean of Wells Cathedral in Somerset. Thus a new Rector, Canon Herbert Hensley Henson, D.D., was appointed in the first year of the new century. In the event and with the historical hindsight, there could have been no better choice.

Twentieth Century

Until the end of the nineteenth century, the day-to-day affairs of the church were the responsibility of the churchwardens, subject at certain periods to resolutions passed at Vestry meetings attended by residents in the parish of St. Margaret's. In 1901, however, the decision was taken to encourage the participation of more active lay members of the church in its affairs. The first Church Council, therefore, came into being 'to meet at various times to discuss various matters concerning the welfare of the Church'. It was stressed that this must in no way encroach on the legal and other exclusive duties appertaining to the office of churchwarden. In keeping with the times, the first Church Council was somewhat less democratic than its more recent successors. It consisted of the rector, churchwardens, clergy, and sidesmen, with six other members to be appointed by the rector and churchwardens. In this context, 'clergy' would probably have the historic definition of 'those with clerkly skills' and would probably include the secretary of the Vestry meetings.

In 1905 work of restoration began at the east end of the church which involved moving the east wall in order to extend the chancel by six feet. Although no official grant has been available from the House of Commons for the upkeep of the fabric of St. Margaret's since the nineteenth century, individual members of the House showed considerable interest in the new project. A special Restoration Committee was set up under the chairmanship of the Rector, Dr Hensley Henson to supervise the work and to raise the necessary finance. Its members at the outset included Mr Speaker Gully during the year which saw his retirement, Sir Michael Hicks-Beach, Mr Asquith, Mr Lyttelton, and certain other Members of the House of Commons who resided in the small area which at that time formed the ecclesiastical parish. Later in the year, on Mr Speaker Gully's retirement, the Rector publicly expressed his thanks for the Speaker's helpful association with the proposal and the early work of restoring the east end of the church. Mr Speaker Gully's place on the Committee was taken by his successor, Mr Speaker Lowther.

Prior to 1909, access to and egress from the church at normal services was only via the North Porch and Door under the tower. As a result of the increasingly large congregations attending these services, considerable congestion was resulting at the time of the congregation's departure, and so it was agreed that when there was a large attendance, the West Door would also be opened to augment the facility of the North Door.

On 19 April 1914, a special House of Commons service was held in St. Margaret's to commemorate the tercentenary of the close relationship that had existed between the House and the church since that first official House of Commons service compulsorily attended by every able bodied Member of Parliament in 1614. Later in 1914, following an assassination in Sarajevo which precipitated the outbreak of the Great War to end all wars, precautions were taken to safeguard the most precious of St. Margaret's treasures. These naturally included the Renaissance glass of the East Window which was removed to a place of safety. By 1916, three choirmen, the Clerk to the Church Council and three sidesmen were all serving their country in Flanders. Not all returned.

On 4 August 1918, at a very critical period in the war, George V and Queen Mary, together with the Members of both Houses or Parliament, attended a special service of intercession at St. Margaret's. The solemn significance of this service was greatly enhanced by the fact that this was the first occasion in English history when a reigning monarch had united with the House of Lords and the House of Commons in an official act of public worship. Three months later, on 11 November, the Prime Minister, David Lloyd George, announced to a crowded House of Commons the conclusion of the Armistice and the details of the terms agreed. Immediately at the end of his statement he added that he felt the occasion was one which called for a special act of thanksgiving to Almighty God. He followed this by suggesting that the House should without delay adjourn to St. Margaret's for this purpose. The proposal was unanimously agreed by the House, and led by Mr Speaker Lowther, the Members left the Chamber and walked across St. Margaret Street to their parish church. There, in a hastily improvised but simple form of service, they were united in an act of praise and thanksgiving. No doubt because of its simple sincerity the service was described by those who attended as 'thrilling and impressive' and as an occasion that 'will never be forgotten by those who took part in it'. In 1919, the East Window was re-erected above the altar.

At a Vestry meeting on 20 May 1926, the Rector, the Revd Carnegie, paid a special tribute to the life and work of the Revd H.F. Westlake who had died on 25 November 1925. He expressed his great appreciation of the work done by H.F. Westlake in his capacity as one of the assistant clergy during the tenure of office of the current rector, and of his predecessor, Dr Hensley Henson. He went on to say that the Revd Westlake had always given of his best whether in ministration or advice to the young and the elderly of St. Margaret's. He also rendered a signal and unique service to St. Margaret's both by his published works and lectures. He is still well known – at the end of the twentieth century – for his history of St. Margaret's Westminster published in 1914. In his preface to the book, H.F. Westlake explains that up to that time, 'With the exception of a short history written by the Revd Mackenzie Walcott, curate of the Church, published by subscription in 1847, and a scanty volume by an old vestryman, Mr W. Bardwell in 1878, nothing but an occasional paper or lecture before a learned society has served to remind the public that St. Margaret's has a history behind it comparable with that of the great Abbey under whose shadow it so literally stands.' His book has stood the test of time for since its publication, apart from references to St. Margaret's in books more broadly based about Westminster, the only specific publications have been a twenty-four page illustrated guide for visitors published in 1973 and a single sheet illustrated guide published in 1983. As a historian he had certainly rendered 'a signal and unique service to St. Margaret's'.

A memorial service for King George V was held in St. Margaret's Church at 2.30 p.m. on Tuesday 28 January 1936 to coincide with the day and the hour of the actual funeral service for the King that was taking place at Windsor. The church was initially reserved for Members and officials of the House of Commons and their wives. They were admitted by the East Door. However, at 2.25 p.m. the North Door was opened to admit members of the general public to fill any pews still remaining unoccupied. The Speaker and members of the Cabinet were unable to be present as they were attending the funeral service at Windsor. Nevertheless, the church was filled to capacity. During the service the choir sang the anthem 'How Blest are They' (Tschaikovsky). Before the address given by the Rector, Canon Carnegie, the congregation joined the choir in singing the hymn 'O God, our help in ages past'. The hymn 'Abide with me' followed the sermon and then after the closing prayer and Benediction, the organ played the 'Dead March in Saul'. Finally the congregation sang the National Anthem.

In 1939, shortly before the declaration of war, the glass of the East Window was again removed and transferred to a studio in Putney for safe keeping. It was recognised that the danger in the coming war would be far greater than it had been in the previous one. Then on Sunday, 3 September 1939, the first day of the Second World War, an air raid warning sounded just as the Rector, the Revd Vernon Faithfull Storr, was entering the pulpit to deliver his sermon. A short pause in the service followed to provide an opportunity for those members of the congregation who wished to leave the church to do so. After they had left, the Rector delivered his sermon and the service continued. At the conclusion of the service the 'all clear' sounded on what had proved to be a false alert. On 9 May 1940 at a Vestry meeting of parish residents it was reported that the outbreak of war had caused many of the congregation to be away from London. The Westminster City School, the source of supply for St. Margaret's choristers, had been evacuated to Tonbridge and Tunbridge Wells. As a result four women had been added to the choir to replace the boys for the first time in St. Margaret's history, and they were being highly successful in maintaining the high standards for which St. Margaret's was noted in this field.

Due to increasing enemy action, Sunday services

had to be discontinued during September 1940. On 25 September, an oil bomb crashed through the roof near the north-west corner of the church causing extensive damage. Apart from setting alight the roof over the North Aisle, it also set on fire a number of pews and caused irreparable damage to a fine monument in memory of one of St. Margaret's much loved parishioners of former times. This was the monument to the Revd James Palmer which had been sited on the north wall. James Palmer was born and lived within the parish, and from 1616 had been the Vicar of St. Brides, Fleet Street until he was compelled to retire through ill health in 1645. As a poorly paid parish priest he had lived frugally, and as a result had managed to accumulate enough capital to endow twelve alms houses for the old, a free school for the young with a commodious habitation for the schoolmaster, and a convenient chapel for prayers and preaching. The school was designed to educate free of charge twenty poor male children born within the parish of St. Margaret. Many years later it was combined with other foundations to create Westminster City School where he is remembered as one of the school's benefactors after whom one of the houses is named. The same bomb also severed the pipe which carried the wind to the organ from the blower in the tower. In the process of extinguishing the flames, water poured into the pipes and effectively put the organ out of action.

Later a high explosive landing in Old Palace Yard effectively destroyed all the windows in the south

The fifteenth century figure of St. Margaret of Antioch

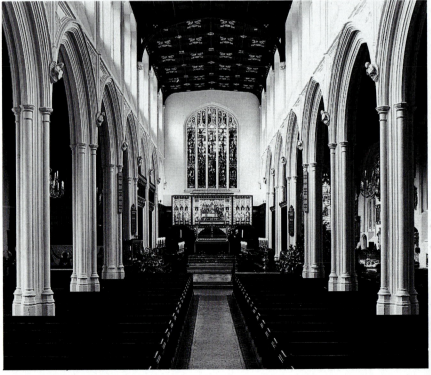

Opposite top: The Supper at Emmaus carved by Seffrin Alken in 1753

Opposite bottom: The Nave and Chancel looking East

Above: Sir Walter Raleigh Memorial Window

Above: John Milton Memorial Window

Opposite top: The Vacher Pulpit

Opposite bottom: The Living Church: Sunday morning at St. Margaret's

Opposite: The Blanche Parry Memorial

Above: The Lady Dorothy Stafford Memorial

Overleaf: St. Margaret's Church, Westminster Abbey

and east walls and two of the windows on the north side of the church. Additionally, all the windows in the clerestory, above the nave and chancel, were severely damaged. One of the windows totally destroyed in the south wall by the bomb aimed at Parliament was a memorial to the first Baron Farnborough, who as Sir Thomas Erskine May was Clerk of the House of Commons from 1871 until 1881. An English constitutional jurist, he became Assistant Librarian in the House of Commons in 1831 and Clerk Assistant in 1856. In 1844, whilst Assistant Librarian, he compiled his *Treatise on the Law, Privileges, Proceedings, and Usage of Parliament*. This has been translated into various languages and is still the standard work on the subject, albeit kept up-to-date by succeeding Clerks of the House as new precedents have been created and new procedures introduced. *Erskine May*, as the book is now known, has become in a secular sense the Bible of the House of Commons. It is an authoritative text book setting out the best codes of practice and behaviour to be followed by all who aspire to become effective parliamentarians.

With the church in such a seriously damaged state it was clearly not practical to hold services during the cold winter weather of 1940–41. However, in his news letter at Easter in 1941, the new Rector announced his firm intention of re-opening the church for services at Whitsuntide and continuing them so long as the weather proved to be not too inclement. Future winter services would have to wait until the very extensive repairs necessary to make the church weatherproof could be effected. At an unusual Vestry meeting of parishioners held on 29 May 1941, the Rector had the sad task of reporting the death in action of Flight Lieutenant John R. Rathbone, MP, who had rendered most valuable service to St. Margaret's during his tenure of office as the People's Churchwarden.

By 1942 the church had been made sufficiently weatherproof to resume Sunday services throughout the seasons. In June 1942, in addition to its own depleted congregation, St. Margaret's was able to accommodate the congregation of a neighbouring damaged church, St. John the Evangelist in Smith Square. Although the East Window had escaped the destruction of the windows in the south and east walls thanks to the prudence of the Rector in having it moved to a studio in Putney in 1939, an offer at this time from London Transport to accommodate it in a disused London Underground station for the rest of the war was gratefully accepted.

In 1943, the ancient ceremony of the Confirmation of Bishops had been due to be held at the church of St. Mary le Bow. Unhappily, enemy action had rendered the church unusable for the purpose and so, for the first time in it's history, St. Margaret's became the venue for this ceremony.

On 8 March 1943, a casket containing the ashes of the Rt. Hon. Captain S.A. Fitzroy, Speaker of the House of Commons from 1928 to 1943, was buried beneath the floor of the chancel in the centre of the choir in the presence of a large and distinguished congregation. The grave was subsequently covered with a stone from the floor of the Chamber of the Commons destroyed by enemy action on 10 May 1941. In 1944 a decision was taken to erect a stained glass window in memory of Captain Fitzroy over the East Porch. It was also decided that the window would display the Arms of Captain Fitzroy together with the Royal Arms and those of the four self-governing Dominions of Australia, Canada, New Zealand and South Africa. This was courageous planning for work to be done after the end of hostilities in the faith that the church would still be in existence at the end of the war, for in 1944 that was by no means sure. In February 1944, St. Margaret's narrowly escaped total destruction when large numbers of incendiary bombs showered down on Parliament Square, New Palace Yard, Old Palace Yard, St. Margaret Street and only feet away from the tower in the churchyard. Many exploded only yards from the north-east corner of the church and a number more close to the north wall. The church was ringed by fire but survived against all the odds.

In 1945 the House of Commons assembled in St. Margaret's to take part in a special service of thanksgiving for the ending of the war with Germany. A later special service of thanksgiving for the Commons marked the ending of the war with Japan.

Earlier faith in the survival of St. Margaret's was seen to be justified on 31 July 1946, when a new window in memory of Mr Speaker Fitzroy was unveiled by the wartime Prime Minister, Mr Winston Churchill. Four and a half months later on 17

December, another moving ceremony took place when the ensign of the escort carrier HMS *Speaker* was dedicated by Captain Fitzroy's successor, Mr Speaker Clifton Brown, at a short ceremony attended by the Ship's Company. The ship's badge and a commemoration plaque were fixed on the wall adjacent to the West Door.

Work on the restoration of the damaged windows in memory of Sir Walter Raleigh and Admiral Blake was completed early in 1947. Later that year the widow of the former People's Churchwarden, Flight Lieutenant John Rankin Rathbone, MP, presented to St. Margaret's a fifteenth century wooden figure of St. Margaret, hands clasped in prayer and, according to tradition, crushing beneath her feet the dragon of evil. This stands on a small table in the sanctuary as a memorial to a gallant airman who gave his life in the defence of freedom. During the war years St. Margaret's Patronal Festival had not taken place for obvious reasons. However, in 1947 St. Margaret's Day, 20 July, coincided with a Sunday and so it seemed to be an appropriate year in which to revive it. This was done.

In 1948, a letter addressed to the Editor of *The Times* launched an appeal for public subscription to meet the cost of restoring the historic Milton window which had been severely damaged by the blast from a high explosive bomb during the war. The cost of the repairs would be £125 but no funds for this particular purpose were available from St. Margaret's own finances. The appeal committee included the Rector, Charles Smyth, T.S. Eliot and

Isaac Foot. The appeal had a quick and ready response and the unveiling ceremony of the restored window took place on 4 July 1949.

On Sunday, 19 June 1949 in place of the 11.00 o'clock service, a sung Eucharist was held according to the form and manner of the service in the Prayer Book of 1549. This was to celebrate the four hundredth anniversary of the Book of Common Prayer. The affection of St. Margaret's congregations for the Book of Common Prayer has remained steadfast, throughout the centuries.

On Remembrance Sunday, 1949, the ship's badge of the aircraft carrier, HMS *Formidable*, and a commemoration plaque were unveiled by Admiral Vian during Evensong.

One year later at morning service, the lessons were read by a grandson of the former Rector of St. Margaret's, Dr Farrar, Field-Marshal Lord Montgomery of Alamein. The rector in his 1951 report to the Vestry meeting revealed that Field Marshal Lord Montgomery returned the compliment by personally entertaining the choristers to tea and to an entertainment given by a conjuror on 8 January 1951.

On 6 November 1952, Queen Elizabeth II, proclaimed but not yet crowned, accompanied by her husband, the Duke of Edinburgh, planted a cross in the British Legion Field of Remembrance in St. Margaret's churchyard. Her Majesty accompanied by the Duke of Edinburgh visited the Field of Remembrance shortly before Remembrance Sunday in subsequent years. Two days after their visit in 1954, at the Remembrance Sunday morning service on 7 November, the lessons were read by Field-Marshal Lord Alexander of Tunis. Gradually the memory of the Second World War and its heroes were fading into history.

In 1955 a lead bust of King Charles I, which had been presented to St. Margaret's by the Society of King Charles the Martyr in 1949, was finally placed in a stone outdoor niche at the eastern end of the church directly facing the statue of Oliver Cromwell across the road on the greensward outside West-minster Hall. In an objective account it would be unseemly to draw any partisan conclusion about the thinking behind this siting of the bust.

At the 1957 Vestry meeting, the Rector, Canon Michael Stancliffe, ended his report with these words: 'My own feeling for what it is worth at the moment, is that the most important thing to be done is to build up a larger congregation and to create in that congregation a corporate sense, so that all may regard themselves as a family, and St. Margaret's as their spiritual home – and not as a church to which they like going but towards the upkeep of which they feel no particular responsiblity.' During 1959, an Association of the Friends of St. Margaret's was founded. The members of this Association included not only regular members of the congregation but also those who, having had some contact with the church in the past, wished to keep in touch with it though no longer living in London. Some thirty years later, although the formal Association no longer exists as such, the strength of the family relationship and acceptance of St. Margaret's as a spiritual home continues to grow on a less formal basis.

Throughout 1961 major works of repair and renewal were carried out at a cost of £5,000 which was met out of church funds with the help of a donation from the British Iron and Steel Federation of £1,500 for the railings. The work included cleaning the interior of the church, renewal of the churchyard railings and stonework, treatment of the roof timber against the deathwatch beetle, and the erection of a new flagpole on the tower.

In 1963, 330 years after the grant of a Royal Charter to the teaching establishment that grew into Westminster City School, the event was marked by a special service in St. Margaret's attended by Her Majesty Queen Elizabeth the Queen Mother.

A Vestry minute records the retirement in July 1965 of St. Margaret's Organist and Choirmaster, Herbert Dawson. He first took up his appointment with St. Margaret's in 1929. At the outbreak of war ten years later, he took leave of absence to join the Royal Air Force. Happily he survived his years in the service, and at the end of hostilites he was able to renew his association with the organ and the choir. During his thirty years in his appointment he established a high reputation for the music of St. Margaret's, which subsequent Directors of Music have sought to maintain.

In the autumn of 1966, new stained glass windows were erected in the south wall to replace all those which had been irreparably damaged as a result of enemy action during the 1939 war. The modern stained glass replacement windows were made by Patrick Reyntiens to the designs of John Piper.

In the twentieth century, the parish of St. Margaret had changed out of all recognition from the thickly populated residential area of the nineteenth century. Not only the slums, but also the upper-class private houses were progressively engulfed by office blocks and other business premises. By the 1950s the parish had virtually ceased to be a residential area. During the next few years it became increasingly apparent that St. Margaret's was becoming no longer financially viable as an independent parish church. So with the prior agreement of Her Majesty the Queen, the Archbishop of Canterbury, the Bishop of London, and the Dean and Chapter of Westminster Abbey, the Westminster Abbey and Saint Margaret Westminster Act 1972 was passed by both Houses of Parliament and came into effect in 1973. Under the terms of the Act, the area of the parish occupied by the Houses of Parliament, the church and its churchyard ceased to be part of the Province of Canterbury, the Diocese and Archdeaconry of London, and of the Rural Deanery of Westminster. The area was added to the Close of Westminster Abbey and now comes under the jurisdiction of the Close with the Dean as the Ordinary, subject only to the jurisdiction of Her Majesty the Queen as the Visitor. The remaining part of the parish outside that area was divided between the parishes of St. Martin-in-the-Fields and St. Matthew Westminster.

In June 1974, the East Window of the church was slightly damaged by the blast of an explosion in

Westminster Hall caused by terrorists of the Irish Republican Army. The damage was repaired and the opportunity was taken to wash the external face of the window and protect it for the future by fitting stainless steel wire guards.

In 1976 the existing solid fuel central heating boiler was replaced by a new gas boiler and was in operation by October of that year. The following year the Dean and Chapter entered into a contract with the original builders of the organ, Messrs J.W. Walker to rebuild it. This now includes a new console in the South Choir Aisle with tracker action and the addition of Spanish trumpets and other modifications.

Mr and Mrs John Elliott of New York City, following the example of Winston Churchill some forty-eight years earlier, were married in St. Margaret's on 27 July 1956 and lived happily ever after. In 1980 they expressed a wish to make a thanksgiving offering for their marriage. The Rector, Canon John Baker, suggested the creation of a chapel in the North Aisle dedicated to Christ the Intercessor and to consist of an altar, candlesticks, altar rails, a hanging backcloth and a new floor. This was approved and work began promptly. The dedication of the new chapel took place on 26 July 1981.

Further damage to windows occurred in 1981 when panes in three of the Piper windows in the South Aisle were damaged by vandals. The first of these was repaired by Patrick Reyntiens who made the original glass, and the other two by Mr A. Fisher of Chapel Studio, Kings Langley.

1984 was the year in which Mr Speaker Weatherill launched his Appeal to raise £900,000 to meet the cost of the repair and restoration of the roof and stonework of St. Margaret's. In the event the Appeal realised £1 million within about twelve months and work was started on the site on 3 March 1986.

November 1984 saw two other projects completed. The first had been set in train in 1977 when Sir Geoffrey de Freitas offered to present to St. Margaret's four sundials to replace the two old clock faces and two windows in the tower. This was to commemorate the association of the House of Commons NATO Committee, of which he was chairman, with St. Margaret's. Final designs of the four dials approved by Sir Geoffrey and the Dean and Chapter were prepared in detail by the sculptor, Edwin Russell and made by Oliver Gero of Brookbrae in time to be fixed in 1982. Unhappily the donor had not lived to see this. An inscription recording Sir Geoffrey's gift was fixed inside the tower, and the final dedication took place on 16 November 1984. On 25 November a memorial plaque in memory of Raymond Gordon, the founder of the Horse Rangers' Association, was unveiled in the south-west corner of the South Aisle behind the font. The plaque was designed and cut in Hopton Wood stone by Mr Arthur Ayres. At the bottom it bears a quotation from Abraham Lincoln: 'A man is never so tall as when he stoops to help a child.' Twice a year some 500 juvenile Horse Rangers attend a special service in St. Margaret's.

The response to Mr Speaker's Appeal for the

repairs to the walls and roof of St. Margaret's arrived at a time of high interest rates. As a result of careful initial investment, therefore, it became possible to raise enough additional funds, with a further limited appeal, to embark on the refurbishment of the interior and the windows of the church. In August 1991 the internal scaffolding was erected and work begun at the east end. By the end of September, it had become necessary to suspend Sunday services in order to expedite the work, as well as to facilitate it in the main body of the church. Careful planning by the architect, Mr Peter Foster, and efficient work by the main contractors, Messrs Rattee and Kett, ensured that the work in the main body of the church was completed by 2 December in time for the service of thanksgiving to be held on 8 December. The work had included lime-washing the stone work, rewiring the electrical circuits and fitting new lighting, cleaning and repairing windows, and cleaning and regilding where necessary the reredos, memorials and monuments.

The thanksgiving service at the conclusion of the work on the interior of the main body of the Church was the second one to be held in 1991. Earlier, on Wednesday, 8 May, a service of thanksgiving for the completion of the restoration of the fabric funded by the Speaker's Appeal for St. Margaret's was held. This was attended by Mr Speaker Weatherill and representatives of all the main contributors to the fund. The service began with a joyful rendition of the hymn 'Now thank we all our God'.

Work on the interior of the tower, following the

precedent set during the major repairs and reconstruction at the beginning of the sixteenth century,
was left until the last and was begun on 10 February
1992. This was completed by mid-June. Whilst the
repair and renovation work was being carried out by
the contractors on the structure, volunteers among
the change ringers carried out necessary work to the
clappers and general maintenance on the bells and
bell frame. The oak frame, which dates from about
1739, was generally in good condition, and cam-
panologists will be interested to know that the bells
form a ring of ten in the key of D.

The early completion of the work on the interior
of the church by the beginning of December 1991
enabled not only the resumption of the regular
Sunday services, but also the traditional Parliamentary Carol Service on Tuesday, 10 December 1991.
This annual event is timed to last for one hour and to
avoid the likelihood of interruption as a result of
votes being taken in the House. The service is shared
with the staff of Westminster Hospital and the
collection is taken in aid of the Westminster Medical
School Research Trust, thus maintaining the long
association between church, hospital and House of
Commons in an unbroken line.

In April 1992 a general election was held and this
was marked by the retirement of Mr Speaker
Weatherill. When the new Parliament assembled,
the House of Commons, for the first time in its
history elected one of the Lady Members to be the
new Speaker. At St. Margaret's, the traditional
service on the occasion of the Opening of Parliament

was held on Thursday, 14 May at 12.00 noon. The service was attended by the Rt. Hon. the Speaker of the House of Commons, Miss Betty Boothroyd, MP, the Lord Chancellor, the Prime Minister and members of the Government, and Members of both Houses of Parliament. The first lesson was read by Madam Speaker, the second by the Lord Chancellor, and the address was given by the Archbishop of Canterbury. Taking part in the service, in addition to the Rector, were the Dean of Westminster, the Roman Catholic Bishop of North London representing the Cardinal Archbishop of Westminster, the Moderator of the Free Church Federal Council, and the Moderator of the General Assembly of the Church of Scotland. The final hymn, sung with great force by the whole congregation, was:

> I vow to thee, my country, all earthly things above,
> Entire and whole and perfect, the service of my love:

The Living Church

Achurch lives through the continuity of corporate worship and the efforts of all those who make a contribution towards sustaining it. Thus, despite the impermanence of man-made structures, St. Margaret's Church has lived for more than 900 years. A church dedicated to St. Margaret of Antioch on this site has been a place of regular worship since it was established by St. Edward the Confessor in the eleventh century. The only breaks, slight in the context of the life of the church, have been for work of reconstruction and refurbishment.

The earliest records show financial support for the church from kings, wool-merchants, artisans and many unidentified citizens of the town of Westminster. Indeed, throughout its history, St. Margaret's has been a focus for the devotion and Christian service given freely by people from all walks of life. The earliest churchwardens' accounts, still in existence, record the list of pew holders in 1460 and 1461. If surnames indicated occupations, as they so often did in the fifteenth century, then these early pewholders included a builder, a wheelwright, a hat maker, a mason, a carpenter, a locksmith and a cobbler. These early pews were generally obtained by the husbands for the use of their wives, and the main part of the floor of the church would have been totally empty of such furniture. In later years, however, the churchwardens' accounts show the provision of increasing numbers of pews indicating the gradual growth towards the present system of providing seating for the whole congregation.

In the late fifteenth and early sixteenth centuries the records list gifts and bequests in great variety and from all kinds of people. Some of them were for specific purposes and some to meet more general expenses of the church. In the churchwardens' accounts covering the years from 1495 to 1497 a large number of gifts and bequests were received from such diverse donors as Sir William Norresse, John Ryman Galand's Father-in-law, the vicar of Chesewyke, Lady Norresse, Thomas Kyte of King's Chapel, a waterman, the Good Wife of the Swan in King Street, Robert Marlow's wife, and many others. Not all gifts and bequests were in cash. In the same period a certain John Amore bequeathed land at Hendon to provide for the upkeep of a lamp in St. Margaret's. Throughout the ages men and women have contributed to the church each in their own way. For many their main contribution has been in time and effort to ensure the beauty, the spirituality and the warmth of fellowship to be found in the church and at the services.

On St. Margaret's Feast Day in 1499 a collection from passers-by during the procession of the virgins through Westminster raised the sum of ten shillings and one penny. The money actually collected by the virgins themselves on that day totalled a further three shillings. The following year among the gifts recorded were six shillings and eightpence from 'My Lord Edmund', the King's third son, as a donation towards the general maintenance fund, and a silver ring, the gift of an old woman, bequeathed to the church by a well wisher. There were many gifts of money at this time to help to pay for the major work of reconstruction which resulted in the building that has, to a great degree, survived to this day. Thus those who are privileged to worship in St. Margaret's today owe a deep debt of gratitude to the many generous parishioners and others who lived during the late fifteenth and early sixteenth centuries and who contributed so much to ensure the survival of the church that has been so well loved down the centuries.

During the early days in the life of St. Margaret's the churchwardens carried very considerable responsibility for raising the revenue and for spending it. The cash they spent did not come solely from collections, gifts and bequests. The records show that an apparently regular income was received from 1467 and for about 100 years afterwards for the provision of pews designated for the exclusive use of the families of particular parishioners. Other regular

sources of income were the facilities available for
burials and marriages, the lease of church land and
the rent from houses owned by the church. During
the period of the early sixteenth-century reconstruction work, there are many entries in the churchwardens' accounts of cash received from wooden
beams, planks, stone and other debris from the
demolition of much of the old church.

Entries of expenditure in the churchwardens'
accounts during this period indicate the wide range
of executive responsibility exercised by them. These
include payments for all the material needed and its
transportation to the site for the great work of
restoration, as well as the employment of skilled
men required to do the work. The entries also show
payments made to preachers, singers and bell-
ringers. They show the cost of vestments purchased,
and of others hired for special occasions. Three
items recorded in 1501 serve to emphasise the variety
of interest covered by the churchwardens' activities.
The first is the payment of four pence for drawing up
a contract between a new clerk on his appointment
and the churchwardens. The second records the
payment of eight pence by the churchwardens to the
keeper of the Abbey vestry for the loan of silk cloths
to cover the High Altar on St. Margaret's Day. The
third item is for the payment of twenty-two pence to
labourers for paving the altar's end in the Lady
Chapel and the Trinity Chapel. All in all, much of
the life of the church and its continuity depended in
those days on the hard work and administrative
talents of the churchwardens.

Later in the sixteenth century, the duties and responsibilities of the churchwardens gradually declined with the advent of the 'Overseers' and the growing power of the 'Vestry'. From the year 1561 until the early years of the twentieth century the records of the overseers, who shared with the churchwardens duties and responsiblities for the care of the poor of the parish of St. Margaret's, are well documented. The parish overseers were established by an Act of Parliament of 1536 which was effectively the beginning of the poor law system. Before this all previous Acts on the subject had aimed only at the repression of mendicancy. The 1536 Act for the first time in our history provided for an actual system of relief through the medium of parochial collections.

The Act sought to discriminate between a deserving beggar and one who had less cause to resort to begging. For the less deserving the existing penalties for begging were extended to include whipping, ear-cropping, and death. However, it became one of the duties of the overseers to distinguish between the beggar worthy of consideration and the beggar who was not. The former would then be licensed and required to wear a pewter ticket on a brass chain to show that their begging was legal. Many of the charitable activities of the church became the responsibilities of the overseer. These included the provision of clothing for the needy, medical attention for sick paupers, the placing of orphans and the burial of those unable to pay for a funeral or grave. It was not considered necessary to provide coffins for such interments, but a winding sheet was provided. Although the charitable work of the church was to a degree formalised by the Act of 1536, it continued to be paid for by those devout Christians who were responsible for transforming a stone edifice into a living church.

The funds administered by the overseers for the relief of the poor came from a wide variety of sources through the agency of the church. Cash and clothing were donated by many of St. Margaret's parishioners, from the Dean of Westminster, from the Royal Maundy Money, and from the knights and the burgesses who were the Members of the House of Commons, and with whom the Abbey and St. Margaret's have always been closely associated. In 1588, for example, the records show that the overseers acknowledged the receipt of seven cloth gowns and six smocks of the total value of four pounds from the Queen's tailor on behalf of Her Majesty. Various other gifts in cash and kind were also acknowledged from Lady Dacre, Lord Burleigh, and Maurice Pickering. Mr Pickering was a regular benefactor in many ways. His valuable contribution to the life of the church was recognised in 1572 on 21 June when he received a patent of the office of 'vergershippe' for the term of his life. Two years later he was authorised to appoint one William Giles to be his deputy in the office of one of the vergers. He served in the office of 'collector' in 1579 and at his death he left the sum of £200 to the parish.

Among the more curious sources of revenue in the parish were the sale of licenses for killing and eating flesh in Lent which were fairly freely available at a price of six shillings and eight pence, and the fines imposed for the non-observance of Sunday. The fines imposed varied considerably depending on the adjudged magnitude of each offence. Two pence was obtained from a woman who committed the crime of selling cherries during the time of a service. On the other hand, certain persons who failed to maintain good order in their houses during service time were fined as much as two shillings and sixpence. One man who sold rotten mutton in the market was fined one shilling, yet another who sold coal at the feast of Candlemas had to pay two shillings and three pence. A trespasser was fined six shillings and eight pence and those who sold strong ale at two pence a quart on 22 March had to pay a fine of three shillings. From the richest to the poorest in the parish who contributed either voluntarily or involuntarily to the revenue and the good works of the church, all participated in breathing life into the church.

Although every church has need of its unsung heroes, its infantry, its backroom boys, who carry out the routine tasks week in and week out, year in and year out, the survival of a vibrant corporate entity through the generations and the centuries has need of much more.

One of the most important effects of the Reformation in the sixteenth and seventeenth centuries was the evolutionary transfer of functions from the ecclesiastical authority to the laity. In the parish of St. Margaret's during the second half of the sixteenth century the householders began to assemble in the vestry. They first established control over the powers of the churchwardens. In 1591 Articles of Agreement were drawn up which resolved that no churchwarden should elect or bring in any man to be a churchwarden unless he had first been selected and elected by the Vestry men, or a majority of them. It was also resolved that the churchwardens should not be allowed to authorise any purchase for the church, or repair to it, that involved the expenditure of more than forty shillings except by a resolution of the Vestry.

Simultaneously the Vestry was assuming control over the paving and cleansing of the streets, the regulation of the activities of beggars, the water supply and many other local government type functions. In time the growth in the development of local government saw the gradual demise of the Vestry as its secular functions were taken over increasingly by elected local authorities. Nevertheless, for nearly 300 years, the Vestry played its part in helping to provide for the needs of the church to maintain it in being. In its day it was a large and important body whose activities were well known and whose intentions were publicly signalled. It could be said therefore to operate in a kind of twilight zone between the unsung backroom boys and the standard bearers in preserving the continuity of the living church.

The standard bearers are those who are heard by the congregation to be making a positive contribution to their corporate worship. In chronological order, these must be the bell-ringers, the sidesmen, the organist or musicians, the singers, the priests and the lay readers. The earliest churches dedicated to St. Margaret would be equipped with a single bell mounted in a frame. The West Tower which was replaced by the present tower at the beginning of the sixteenth century had three bells and a frame. When the present tower was built these were installed in the new tower together with two new bells cast by William Smith to establish a new ring of five. According to the churchwardens' accounts of 1527, the weight of the tenor was 16cwt 0qr 13lb. So the present day St. Margaret's Society of Change Ringers has a long tradition behind it of calling the faithful to worship and of expressing great joy and great sadness whenever the occasion demanded it.

For nearly 500 years St. Margaret's peals have punctuated the pages of our island's history. On only one occasion do the ringers appear to have failed in their duty with what could have been dire consequences. The churchwardens' accounts show that on 2 July 1548 the sum of two shillings and four pence had to be paid to the King's Almoner to dissuade him from sealing up the doors of the church because the church bells had not been rung during the visit of the boy King Edward VI on that day. Otherwise their record has been impeccable.

On 7 August 1596 the bells pealed for joy of victory against the Spaniards, and the bell-ringers received the sum of seven shillings and six pence for their efforts. During the twelve months from May 1606 until May 1607, the records show many special occasions when the bells were rung. These included the celebration of the birth of the King's child, and shortly afterwards the occasion of the visit of James I to London. Then on 4 August 1606 the bells rang to welcome the King of Denmark on his visit to the Abbey, and this was followed by a further peal on 5 August in honour of King James' Day. The bells rang out again on the first anniversary of the failure of the gunpowder plot, 5 November 1606, and they also rang in honour of the King's coronation day. On 5 August 1608 they again pealed out to celebrate the failure of the plot to assassinate King James by the Earl of Gowrie. These are just a small sample of the historic occasions when the bells of St. Margaret's rang out in addition to the regular parochial occasions and the not infrequent parliamentary occasions during the life of the church.

If there are any unsung heroes among the 'standard bearers' they must be the sidesmen. They are the first people to greet visitors at the church when they arrive to attend morning service. They distribute the books required by members of the congregation for the service, and then recover them and put them away at the end of the service. They are responsible for making collections during the service. They ensure that they are strategically dispersed throughout the body of the church so that they are readily available to act promptly should an emergency occur during the service. In short, they play a vital role in ensuring that members of the congregation shall feel welcome and shall know what is expected of them throughout the service. They are a band of people devoted to their church who seek no reward for their time and effort other than the satisfaction that comes from being of service. It is hardly surprising that references to sidesmen in the old records of St. Margaret's and the early church-wardens' accounts are few and far between. They do, however, occur enough to confirm that sidesmen for many centuries have been making their contribution towards the maintenance of corporate worship in St. Margaret's. For the visitation of the Archdeacon in 1561 it is recorded that eleven pence was spent on providing food and drink for the wardens and sidesmen who were to be presented to him. In 1604 ten shillings and ten pence were paid to 'the Ordinarie for the Churchwardens Oathe, and the Sidemens and for the Thirty three Articles'. Two years later the charge for the oaths for 'the Churchwardens and Sidesmens' was still ten shillings and ten pence.

There is no record of the installation of the first organ in St. Margaret's, but in the churchwardens' accounts of 1474 there is a reference to the mending of the 'small Organs and Wall Organ'. Five years later there is a reference to the organist, Matthew Metyngham who was paid eight pence for playing at the organ 'when we had butte one clerk'. History does not record which of the organs was played by Matthew Metyngham on that occasion, but one year later the small organ had to be repaired at a cost to the churchwardens' fund of twelve shillings.

Confirmation of the long line of organists who served St. Margaret's well throughout its continuing life of corporate worship is freely given by the regular payments for the repair and maintenance of successive organs. In 1486, the bellows of the organ in the rood-loft had to be repaired at a cost of six pence. On St. Margaret's Day in the year 1509, some weeks after the coronation of King Henry VIII, it was decided to borrow the organs from the Abbey. The cost of transporting them from the Abbey to St. Margaret's and back was two pence. In 1510 Canon Sir Richard Ede both sang and played the organs at services throughout the year. Further repairs were needed to the organs in 1562 and again in 1586 and 1587. Early in 1596, replacement organs were acquired from the Abbey and the churchwardens were instructed to get the best price they could for the old ones for the benefit of the parish. However, by the year 1613 repairs were needed for the replacement organs. To the present day, the great contribution of organ music to the worship in St. Margaret's continues to be punctuated by break-downs and repairs.

In 1523 the excellent contribution made by a local fishmonger, Adam Swayne, towards helping and maintaining 'God's service in the Choir' was recognised and thoroughly appreciated by the senior members of the church, or, as they are described in the records, divers of the Worshipful of the parish. In recognition of his devoted and successful efforts to maintain the quality of the singing over a period of six months, he was awarded the princely sum of thirteen shillings and four pence.

In most churches a more traditional way of expressing appreciation for special efforts by choristers is by means of the choir supper. In this respect, for much of its history St. Margaret's has been no exception, though the nature of 'supper' provision has varied with the passage of time. In 1478 only wine was provided for the choir men on Corpus Christi Day. In 1481 visiting singers from the King's Chapel were supplied with wine on the eve of St. Margaret's Day. More wine was provided in the rood-loft for them in the morning and then after Evensong on the same day, they were supplied with more wine at a local hostelry. Their throats were clearly well lubricated throughout the feast of St. Margaret.

In 1485 the choir from King's Chapel again sang at St. Margaret's on Corpus Christi Day, but on this occasion they were regaled with bread, ale and wine. Later in the same year on St. Margaret's Day, the choir again received bread, ale and wine. This continued to be the choir's standard form of refreshment until 1545 when the 'menu' included bread, ale, beer and wine. This in fact was the standard fare offered to almost all who visited St. Margaret's on official duties during the second half of the sixteenth century, including the Dean of Westminster. Only in the case of the King's Visitors was it deemed appropriate to add 'an honest dish of meat' to the wine, and for the Archdeacon's Vistitation he, and other important people involved in the Vistitation, enjoyed a dinner which was debited in the churchwardens' accounts in 1562 at forty-two shillings and eight pence. During the seventeenth century the choirs of both St. Margaret's and the Abbey took over responsiblity for their annual feasts to both of which the churchwardens of St. Margaret's made a financial contribution from the wardens' fund. This practice has ceased with the passage of time, but the choir and accompanying organ continue to provide music of a very high standard.

Spiritual leadership and care for the spiritual needs of the people have always rested primarily on the shoulders of the local priests and this has usually included the nature and conduct of corporate worship. During the years of the first St. Margaret's Church, the Abbot of the Benedictine monastery of St. Peter, now Westminster Abbey, was the Rector of St. Margaret's and he would have appointed monks as chaplains to be responsible for the regular services in the church. An accurate record of the names of the clergy attached to St. Margaret's has been maintained from the reign of Henry III in an unbroken line until the present day. From the middle of the thirteenth century until early in the fifteenth century, only a single Christian name is recorded for each of the chaplains apart from the one exception of Thomas de Cherlecote who served for a fifty-year period from 1316 until 1366. The last of the 'chaplain' appointments was made in 1484. He was William Kempston who was replaced in 1497 by Sir William Morowe, appointed as the 'Masse Priest'. It should be explained that the prefix 'Sir' applied to a priest, until well into the seventeenth century, indicated that its owner did not possess a university degree.

Sir William Morowe's successor in 1503 was Sir John Conyers who was the first Curate of St.

Margaret's. Although most appointments from then until 1840 were either 'curates' or 'ministers', there were notable exceptions. In 1640 a Lecturer, Mr Stephen Marshall whose antipathy to Charles I was well known, was appointed to preach on two occasions at House of Commons services in St. Margaret's. The Curate of the church appointed by the Dean and Chapter of Westminster Abbey was a Dr Gilbert Wymberley who also held the office of Lecturer. In 1641, the House of Commons recommended to the Vestry that Mr Marshall should be appointed as their lecturer. The Vestry minutes record that this was done in the presence of Dr Wymberley who promptly resigned. Mr Marshall continued in his post until the following year, 1642. Then, by order of the House, Mr Samuel Gibson, B.D. a learned and orthodox divine was installed as the new Curate of St. Margaret's. The House again intervened in St. Margaret's affairs in 1657 when it made representations to Oliver Cromwell to terminate the appointments of Mr Vyner and Mr Warmstree as Curate and Lecturer at St. Margaret's. This was done and they were replaced by a minor Canon of the Abbey, Dr William Tucker.

The increasing prestige of those priests appointed to St. Margaret's was already becoming apparent by this time. Dr William Outram, who served St. Margaret's from 1664 until 1679, was also Prebendary of Westminster from 1664 and Archdeacon of Leicester from 1669 until 1679. His successor, Dr Thomas Sprat was Chaplain to the King, Prebendary of Westminster, and Canon of Windsor before relinquishing his appointment at St. Margaret's to become first the Dean of Westminster and in addition the Bishop of Rochester. In 1724 the former Dean of both Peterborough and Lincoln, Dr Edward Gee became the Curate and remained in his appointment until his death in 1730. He was assisted in his duties at St. Margaret's by Richard Widmore who was Librarian to the Dean and Chapter of Westminster Abbey, and an author of a history of the Abbey.

Dr Scawen Kenrick combined his office as Curate of St. Margaret's with that of Chaplain to the House of Commons from 1730 until 1753. Until 1734 he was also Prebendary of Westminster Abbey. He then became Archdeacon and later the Subdean. In 1835 Henry Hart Milman, M.A. was appointed curate of St. Margaret's and in 1840 became its first individual rector. A distinguished scholar he was a Fellow of Brasenose, the Professor of Poetry at Oxford in 1821, Bampton Lecturer in 1827, author of *The History of the Jews*, *The History of Christianity* and a number of hymns which included 'Ride on, ride on in Majesty'. He ceased to be the Rector in 1849 to take up his appointment as Dean of St. Pauls. He was succeeded in 1849 by William Cureton, D.D., the author of a classified catalogue of Arabic manuscripts in 1846, and the discoverer of the Epistles of Ignatius.

Doctor Frederic William Farrar became the Rector in 1876 and then, after nine years in the service of St. Margaret's, resigned in order to become the Dean of Canterbury. Doctor Joseph

Armitage Robinson was the Rector for only three years from 1899, and was then transferred to the Abbey to become the Dean of Westminster. Nine years later he became the Dean of Wells Cathedral. His successor, Dr Hensley Henson, after twelve years as Rector of St. Margaret's and two as Subdean of Westminster, became the Dean of Durham.

A new pattern of responsibility for the Rector of St. Margaret's began to emerge with the appointment of Canon Carnegie of Westminster Abbey in 1913. Three years later he became also Chaplain to the Speaker of the House of Commons. From 1916 until 1936 he continued to wear three hats as a member of the Chapter of Westminster Abbey, the Rector of St. Margaret's, and Chaplain to Mr. Speaker. His successor Alan Campbell Don took a slightly different route to the three hats. He was appointed first to be the Speaker's Chaplain in 1936 and then in 1941 he was installed as a Canon of Westminster and shortly afterwards appointed as Rector of St. Margaret's. Although the relationship between church and Abbey has stayed firm, the rectors in office between 1946 and 1961 did not become chaplains to Mr Speaker. However, since 1961 five rectors, all members of the Westminster Abbey Chapter, have been appointed by each of the Speakers since that date to be their chaplains. Of the five, one subsequently became the Bishop of Salisbury, two became the Dean of Winchester – consecutively – one became Dean of Norwich, and the Rector appointed in 1987, Dr Donald Gray, was already a distinguished academic, author, historian and member of the Liturgical Commission. He also brought with him a wealth of experience as a parish priest, Rural Dean, and Chaplain to the Queen. The spiritual leadership and the quality of public worship is being maintained at such a high level that, even without the lay support provided by a parish, there is no shortage of Christians ready to play a part in support as servers, lay readers, crucifers and sidesmen simply because they love St. Margaret's and are proud to be a part of its fellowship.

That has always been the foundation of the living church. It is as true today at St. Margaret's as it has ever been throughout its history, but now, thanks to the ease of long distance travel, those Londoners who are able to serve their church week in week out are well supported by others from all parts of the world in sustaining its heartbeat.

The Good and the Great

The first recorded Chaplain of St. Margaret's was Brother Simon. He was a Benedictine monk from the Westminster monastery appointed by the Abbot of Westminster to provide pastoral care and the facilities for corporate worship to the people of the surrounding neighbourhood. The actual date of his appointment is not known precisely, but it would be either late in the reign of King John or in the opening years of the reign of his successor, King Henry III. As a Benedictine monk he lived a life of total dedication to his Lord and Master, Jesus Christ, and as the member of the order selected to be the Chaplain of St. Margaret's Church by his Abbot he would need to be a man of strong conviction and steadfast faith. During the turbulent reign of Henry III, Simon was succeeded by two other appointees of the Abbot, Brothers Robert and Alexander. There is then a gap in the records until 1316, when Thomas de Cherlecote was appointed. He remained in the appointment for fifty years after which three more members of the Benedictine order,

Brothers William, Ralph and William continued to lead the congregations until early into the fifteenth century.

The strength of corporate worship in St. Margaret's and the unwavering support of succeeding generations that have enabled it to keep the faith, to survive and to flourish through all the vicissitudes of the succeeding centuries is founded on the spirituality of these early good men. Perhaps it is no coincidence that the earliest known Chaplain of St. Margaret's was named Simon, and the monastery which nurtured it during its early years was dedicated to St. Peter.

Appreciation of the splendid efforts of the main body of good and devout Christians who have sustained the living church through the ages need not detract from a natural pride in the fame or good works achieved by individual members of St. Margaret's fellowship throughout its long history. One of the earliest parishioners to find a unique place in English history was undoubtedly Geoffrey Chaucer. He was born in or about the year 1345. He was the son of a vintner and tavern keeper, John Chaucer, who lived in the parish and who was probably a deputy to the King's butler. In the year 1359, at the age of about fourteen, he served in the campaign in France and was taken prisoner at Réthel. However, he was soon ransomed and the early records show that Edward III made a contribution of sixteen pounds towards the amount demanded for his release. In 1368 Geoffrey Chaucer was appointed to be one of the King's Esquires, and his wife Philippa became one of the Ladies of the Queen's Bedchamber. The following year he achieved recognition as a poet with his *Book of the Duchess* on the death of John of Gaunt's wife. During the next ten years he made a number of trips abroad in the King's service and became Comptroller of the Customs and Subsidy of Wools, Skins and Tanned Hides in the port of London. He later became Comptroller of the Petty Customs and in 1386 he was elected a knight of the shire of Kent. By this time he was devoting more time to writing and his *Prologue to the Canterbury Tales* was completed in 1387.

The prologue has been described as a piece of descriptive writing unique in all literature for its variety, grace, humour and comprehensiveness. Chronologically, Chaucer is undoutedly the first great English poet. In order of merit he certainly ranks among the first of all our poets. It was during these years that his genius was at its brightest. For the last year of his life he lived in a small house situated between St. Margaret's and the Abbey. He died on 25 October 1440, and was buried in the part of Westminster Abbey that later became known as Poets' Corner because of his burial there.

Unlike Chaucer, Caxton was not a native of London. He was born at Tenterden in the Weald of Kent. After serving an apprenticeship with a London mercer, Robert Large, he made his home in Bruges where, from 1462 until 1470, he was acting Governor of the English Nation, that is to say, of the Company of Merchant Adventurers. He had diplomatic dealings with Burgundy and the Hanse and then in 1471 he attached himself to the household of the Duchess of Burgundy who was a sister of Edward IV. He learnt the art of printing whilst in Cologne at about this time. Then in Bruges during the years 1474 and 1475 he put through the press there the first book printed in the English tongue, which was called the *Recuyell of the Historyes of Troye*. Another of his early publications produced in Bruges was *The Game and Playe of the Chesse*. It was not until 1476 at the age of fifty-four that he returned to England and set up his wooden press in Tothill Street close to St. Margaret's. He continued to live and work there right up to the time of his death in 1492, when, like his father before him, he was buried in the churchyard of St. Margaret's.

St. Margaret's literary associations which began with Geoffrey Chaucer were continued in the late fifteenth and early sixteenth centuries through its connection with John Skelton, the Poet Laureate of his day. He studied at Cambridge and probably Oxford as well before becoming tutor to Prince Henry, and later the rector of Diss. He was eventually suspended for breaking his vow of celibacy. In 1489 Skelton had produced some translations and elegies, but then began to strike an original vein of satirical vernacular poetry heavily spiced with grotesque words and images and unrestrained jocularity. Typical of these were *The Bowge of Courte*, *Colyn Cloute*, and *Why come ye nat to Courte*. The first of these was an allegorical poem; the second an unsparing attack on the corruption to be found in the Church; however, the third was more specific, containing sustained invective against Cardinal Wolsey for which Skelton was forced to take sanctuary in Westminster Abbey. He died in 1529 and was buried at St. Margaret's which had been his parish church during his later years.

The association of St. Margaret's with the English dramatist Nicholas Udall lasted for the final fifteen years of his life until 1556 when he was buried in the churchyard. He was born in Hampshire and educated at Winchester and Oxford. In 1534, at the early age of thirty, he became Headmaster of Eton. He published a selection from Terence, *Flowers of Latin Speaking*, for his pupils who, however, soon became painfully aware of his predilection for corporal punishment. He was dismissed from Eton in 1541 for indecent offences but this in no way affected his standing at Court. Edward VI thereafter appointed him Prebendary of Windsor, and despite his unbridled enthusiasm for the Reformation he managed to survive the reign of Queen Mary without disfavour. In his later years, Nicholas Udall was responsible for a translation of Erasmus and of selections from the Great Bible. He also translated Latin commentaries on the Great Bible, but he is chiefly remembered as the author of a rollicking comedy *Ralph Roister Doister*, which was to have considerable influence on later English writers of comedies. It was inspired by his favourite classical writers Plautus and Terence, and was completed three years before his death. Unfortunately, he did not survive to see it published in 1567.

It has been wisely said that the memorial window to Sir Walter Raleigh rightly implies that he was an outstanding Elizabethan who had the misfortune to live longer than the Queen. A man of many parts, he was soldier, courtier, navigator and author. He gained his early military experience fighting in France at Jarnac and Moncontour as a volunteer in the Huguenot cause. His introduction to navigation and exploration came in 1578 when he joined the ill-fated expedition led by his half-brother, Sir Humphrey Gilbert, 'to discover and occupy remote heathen lands'. The expedition, frustrated by dissension, tempests, and an unhappy brush with the Spaniards, cost Gilbert his own and his wife's estates. On his return in 1580, Raleigh took a troop of a hundred foot soldiers to Ireland to act against the rebels. This he did with great dash and daring. When he returned to England a year later he entered the Court as a protégé of the Earl of Leicester. As Captain of the Guard, he quickly became a favourite of the Queen who bestowed upon him estates, the 'farm of wines', and a licence to export woollen broadcloths. He was knighted in 1584 and in the following year he was appointed Vice-admiral of Devon and Cornwall and entered Parliament to represent Devon.

A fleet he sent out to explore the American coast north of Florida took possession of an area to which Queen Elizabeth was pleased to approve the name of Virginia. During the following two years Raleigh spent £40,000 on two further expeditions to Virginia but the only results of these were the introduction of potatoes and tobacco into England. In 1587, displaced in the Queen's favour by the handsome young Earl of Essex, he moved to Ireland where he owned 42,000 acres in Munster. Here he set about re-peopling the area with English settlers and became a firm friend of the poet, Edmund Spenser. He grew tobacco and potatoes on his land and wrote the poem *The Ocean's Love to Cynthia* (Elizabeth). He quickly recovered his influence at Court and resumed his plans for the discomfiture of the Spaniards. In 1591 he published his famous account of the fight of the *Revenge* which was the inspiration for Tennyson's noble ballad on the subject. In July 1592 he was committed to the Tower after the Queen had discovered his intrigue with one of her maids-of-honour, Bessie Throgmorton. Released from the Tower later in the year, he married Bessie Throgmorton and for the next two years they lived together in quiet happiness in the town of Sherborne.

In 1595 with a small expeditionary force of five ships Raleigh explored the coasts of Trinidad and sailed up the Orinoco River. Early in the following year he published *The Discovery of Guiana*. Then in June he sailed with Howard and Essex to Cadiz and it was his advice that governed that outstanding victory. Again, his account of the action, published under the title *Relation of Cadiz Action* remains the best history of the exploit. In 1597, he was allowed to resume his former Court appointment as Elizabeth's Captain of the Guard. In 1600, he became Governor of Jersey where, in the space of three years, he did much to foster its trade. After the death of his Queen in 1603, her successor King James, his mind poisoned by Raleigh's enemies at Court, had Raleigh arrested and tried at Winchester where he was condemned to death. On the scaffold, his sentence was commuted to perpetual imprisonment. During his incarceration he occupied his time in writing. He completed volume one of his *History of the World*, *The Prerogative of Parliaments*, *The Cabinet Council* and *A Discourse of War*. Then, on 30 January 1616, he was released from prison to make an expedition up the Orinoco in search of gold. He set sail in April 1617 but the expedition failed and, on his return in June 1618, Raleigh was arrested. The sentence of death passed on him at Winchester fifteen years earlier was duly carried out in Old Palace Yard almost within the shadow of St. Margaret's where his remains lie buried in a place of honour beneath the altar. In his life, Sir Walter Raleigh was a man of great courage and resource. He was a hard-working, God-fearing Christian Protestant who achieved success as a soldier, sailor, farmer and administrator. St. Margaret's *habitués* have cause to be well satisfied that their forbears treated him in death with the honour that was so well merited.

The year 1614 was the year in which St. Margaret's became the House of Commons' Church when, for the first time, the Commons attended St. Margaret's *en masse* in its official capacity to receive the Holy Communion. It was in the same year that John Pym first entered Parliament when he was returned as the Member for Calne in Wiltshire. Eleven years later he exchanged his seat for Tavistock. He joined the

Country Party and waged a personal war against such issues as monopolies, papistry, the Spanish match, and absolutism with a tenacity of purpose that earned him a three months' prison sentence. In 1626, Pym played a major role in the Commons impeachment of the Duke of Buckingham who was saved only by the dissolution of Parliament. In the Parliament of 1628 he was second only to Sir John Eliot in supporting the Petition of Right. On 11 November 1640, Pym named Thomas Wentworth, Earl of Strafford as the 'principal author and promoter of all those counsels which had exposed the kingdom to so much ruin'. Strafford was impeached and placed on trial in March 1641 when Pym acted as the principal prosecutor. When it became clear that the Commons might well fail to obtain a conviction, Pym asked for an adjournment to give the Commons time to pass a Bill of Attainder, which, with the assent of the House of Lords, effectively declared Strafford guilty by Act of Parliament. He was executed on 12 May 1641.

John Pym continued to play a leading role in every other crisis between King and Parliament until the outbreak of civil war became inevitable. He was one of the named five members singled out by King Charles when he entered the Commons in his unsuccessful attempt to have them seized. Later in 1642, when hostilities broke out, Pym remained in London as a member of the executive to perform a service for the Parliamentarian cause no less essential than that of a general in the field. In 1643 he was appointed to be Lieutenant of the Ordnance, and died one month later. He was not by nature a revolutionary, but was said to be, in intellectual terms, very conservative. He was, however, totally dedicated to the cause of what he believed to be the ancient constitution. By his understanding of the term, he was a good 'House of Commons' man'. After his death, with the Parliamentary army in control of London, he was buried with all honours in Westminster Abbey. After the Restoration, the bodies of all the heroes of the Commonwealth period, including that of Pym, were exhumed from their graves in the Abbey and reburied in St. Margaret's churchyard. In the event, this was a more appropriate resting place for John Pym since, during the period of his life in London, he had been a not infrequent worshipper in St. Margaret's and would certainly have been more familiar with the inside of the church than he was with the Abbey.

A member of St. Margaret's congregation who, unlike John Pym, fared badly during the Commonwealth but, in the main, prospered thereafter was the son of a London tailor, Samuel Pepys. The parish register of 1655 records his marriage in St. Margaret's at the age of twenty-two years. He lived in poverty during the early years of his marriage, but after the Restoration, through the patronage of his father's cousin the Earl of Sandwich, he rose rapidly in the naval service. He is especially remembered for two achievements. The first was his reorganisation at the Admiralty which greatly improved the efficiency of the navy, and the second was his famous diaries which added so much detail to our knowledge of history between 1 January 1660 and 31 May 1669. The diaries give a vivid account of contemporary life including naval administration and Court intrigues. They are of special interest to historians because of the details given of the three great disasters of that decade: the Great Plague, the Fire of London and the Dutch Fleet sailing up the Thames. His diaries ended in the year that his wife died and his eyesight failed.

In 1673, Pepys became Secretary of the Admiralty but lost his office in 1679 because of his alleged complicity in the Popish Plot. However he was reinstated five years later and in the same year became President of the Royal Society. Apart from the historical importance of his diaries, they are of extraordinary interest as the personal record of a man of abounding love of life. They also reveal that he regularly attended St. Margaret's, though perhaps not always drawn by the need to share in corporate worship. For example, he confesses that on Sunday, 26 May 1667 he pursued Mrs Martin to the church, and being offered by Mr Howlett a pew in the gallery 'did entertain myself with my perspective glass up and down the church, by which I had the pleasure of seeing and gazing at a great many very fine women: and what with that, and sleeping, I passed away the time till sermon was done, and then to Mrs Martin . . .' He did, however, normally listen to the sermons of which he was something of a connoisseur. It was in St. Margaret's on Sunday, 13 May 1666 that he reports having heard 'a young man play the foole upon the doctrine of purgatory'.

A contemporary of Samuel Pepys, though twenty-five years older than he, was John Milton, who returned to London in 1639 after an absence of some years spent in Cambridge and Italy. He settled in the parish of St. Margaret's and undertook the education of his two nephews. However, two years later he emerged as the polemical champion of the Puritan cause in a series of pamphlets against episcopacy. In 1643 he launched his second series of controversial pamphlets on the subject of divorce. These were occasioned by the refusal of his wife, formerly Mary Powell, the daughter of a royalist, whom he had married earlier that year, to return to him after visiting her parents. The first of these was *The Doctrine and Discipline of Divorce* which, in 1643, involved him in three supplementary pamphlets against the opponents of his views on the subject. These pamphlets occasioned a threat of prosecution by a parliamentary committee which was dominated by the Presbyterians who now shared with the episcopacy the main opposition to his views. His wife returned to him in 1645 accompanied by her whole family as refugees and two years later, subsidised by a legacy from his father, he was able to give up teaching and devote himself to his writing. His pamphlet *The Tenure of Kings and Magistrates in defence of the Regicides* published in 1649 earned him the role of official apologist for the Commonwealth.

His wife, Mary, died in 1652 leaving him with three daughters. In 1651 they had moved to 'a pretty garden house' in the street that is still known as Petty

France. In 1652 the banns of marriage between John Milton and Catherine Woodcock were called in St. Margaret's although, in accordance with the wishes of Parliament, the ceremony took place before a magistrate on 12 November 1656. In their home in Petty France they were blissfully happy for fifteen months. Then Catherine died giving birth to their first child, a daughter, who survived her mother by only six weeks. Both mother and daughter were buried in St. Margaret's churchyard. By this time, Milton's sight had failed completely and he expressed his grief at his bereavement and his blindness in a most beautiful and pathetic sonnet written shortly after Catherine's death:

> Methought I saw my late espoused saint . . .
> Come vested all in white, pure as her mind.
> Her face was veiled, yet to my fancied sight
> Love, sweetness, goodness in her person shined
> So clear as in no face with more delight.
> But O as to embrace me she inclined,
> I waked, she fled, and day brought back my night.

After the Restoration, Milton went into hiding for a short time and then for the remainder of his life he devoted himself to writing poetry. He married his third wife, Elizabeth Minshull, in 1662 and they lived together in what is now called Bunhill Row until his death in 1674.

The English political theorist, James Harrington, although a republican, became a personal attendant of Charles I in 1646 and three years later accompanied him to the scaffold. He lived for much of his adult life in the parish of St. Margaret's. His semi-romance *Oceana* was completed in 1656. In it he set forth a commonwealth and maintained that the real basis of power is property, especially landed property, from which no one person should derive more than £3,000 a year. He also asserted that the rulers should be changed every three years and their successors elected by ballot. In 1661 he was arrested for attempting to change the constitution, and when in prison he went temporarily insane. After his release he returned to live in the parish for the rest of his life. He died in 1677 and was buried at St. Margaret's under the chancel near the remains of Sir Walter Raleigh and the University Poet Laureate, John Skelton. In the light of the preoccupation of the churchwardens with the development of education in Westminster, one passage at least in the *Commonwealth of Oceana* would have endeared James Harrington to St. Margaret's. It reads: 'A Man is a Spirit rais'd by the Magic of Nature; if she doese not stand safe, and so that she may set him to some good and useful work, he spits fire and blows up Castles, for where there is life, there must be motion or work; and the work of idleness is mischief, but the work of industry is health. To set Men to this, the Commonwealth must begin betimes with them, or it will be too late; and the means whereby she sets them to it is EDUCATION, the plastic art of Government.'

Among those who began their Christian lives at

the font in St. Margaret's were the statesman Lord Liverpool and the arbiter of fashion George Bryan Brummell, more popularly remembered as 'Beau'. Robert Banks Jenkinson, the son of the first Lord Liverpool was baptized in St. Margaret's, the House of Commons' Church, in 1770, and entered the House of Commons as the Member for Rye in 1791. He was a Tory with Liberal ideas on trade and finance. In 1801, as Foreign Secretary, he negotiated the Treaty of Amiens. He was subsequently Home Secretary during the last years of Pitt's administration. After the death of William Pitt in 1806, he declined to form an administration and returned to the Home Office. During Spencer Perceval's administration in 1809, having the year previously inherited the title from his father, Lord Liverpool was Secretary for War and the Colonies. In 1812, after the dramatic assassination of Spencer Perceval in the Commons debating Chamber, he agreed to form the new government which continued in office for nearly fifteen years. During his period in office his financial policy was considered to be generally sound, enlightened, and economical, and he succeeded in uniting the old and the new Tories at a critical period. In February 1827 he was struck down with apoplexy and died the following year.

Beau Brummel, christened George Bryan at St. Margaret's in 1778, was the grandson of a 'Gentleman's Gentleman' and the son of Lord North's private secretary. At Eton, and during a short stay at Oxford, he was more distinguished for his dress and manners than for his academic prowess. On leaving

Oxford, he spent four years in the army before inheriting a fortune which enabled him to follow his natural vocation as an arbiter of fashion and elegance. However, the pace began to tell, and his wit became too sharp for his patron and admirer of twenty years' duration, the Prince Regent. They quarrelled in 1813 and in 1816 Brummell's mounting gambling debts forced him to flee to Calais. For fourteen years he struggled to survive in Calais as recklessly as before, then from 1830 until 1832 he held a sinecure appointment as the British Consul at Caen. In 1837 he was committed to a pauper lunatic asylum in Caen where, after three years of imbecility, he died.

In 1908, the year in which he became President of the Board of Trade, Winston Churchill married Clementine Ogilvy Hozier, the second daughter of Sir Henry and Lady Blanche Hozier, and the grand-daughter of the Earl of Airlie. The marriage took place in St. Margaret's on 12 September and was widely regarded as the society wedding of the year; in Churchill's own words he 'lived happily ever after'. His bride was a very remarkable lady. She was an indefatigable worker for charitable causes. She organised canteens for munitions workers during the First World War and the Red Cross Aid to Russia fund during the Second. She served on many committees and held honorary degrees from Oxford and Glasgow Universities. She was created a C.B.E. in 1918 and a life Peer in 1965 when she took the title of Baroness Spencer-Churchill of Chartwell.

Winton Churchill after a very full life as soldier,

journalist, politician, and statesman, regarded May 1940 when power slipped from the hands of Neville Chamberlain, as the time when he began his 'walk with destiny'. During the Second World War as Prime Minister he worked round the clock, travelled 150,000 miles and was constantly under decision-making pressure from shaping the Atlantic Charter in 1941 and devising the strategy for the Western Desert in 1942, to coping with all the pressures arising from the Battle of the Atlantic and the *Luftwaffe* raids on Britain. He developed a close personal relationship with the President of the USA whilst maintaining an often difficult alliance with the USSR. Throughout, he continued to give support and encouragement to the people of defeated nations in Europe. He had a rich and vivid, though intensely human, personality whose abiding qualities included courage and imagination, passion and magnanimity in the service of an unfailing patriotism, yet he always regarded himself, in his own words, as 'a child of the House of Commons'. By the same token, the Commons' Church, wherein he embarked on fifty-seven years of a happily married life with Clementine, was always assured of a warm place in his affections. After his death in 1965 he lay in state in Westminster Hall just across the street from the altar of St. Margaret's before which he and his bride had made their marriage vows.

The Parliamentary Link

Whilst Sunday, 17 April 1614 was the first time that the House of Commons, as a corporate body, had taken communion in St. Margaret's it was just the starting point on the long road that the Commons and its church have travelled together ever since. The early records are not sufficiently complete to show whether a Communion of all the members at their newly 'adopted' church became an annual event or not. Nevertheless, the irregularity of such reports as are available are no proof that the attendances at St. Margaret's were other than at regular intervals. For example the parish records show that on 3 July 1618 forty-seven pounds, five shillings and eight pence were 'received of the Right Honourable the Commons House of Parliament, when they took the Communion in the parish church'. After the reports in the Commons' Journals of 1620 concerning whether or not Dr Ussher should be allowed to preach at the Commons' Communion service in February of that year, the Journal of the House remained silent on the subject for some years afterwards. However, the church-wardens' accounts proved to be more informative. In the accounts of 1626 it is recorded that the sum of fifty-two pounds and twelve shillings was received 'of the Right Honourable House of Commons at several times when they received the Communion at the parish church' in the first and second years of the reign of Charles I.

In the following year the churchwardens' accounts show an expenditure of five pounds and seventeen shillings 'for bread and wine, when the Right Honourable the Commons House of Parliament received the Communion in the parish church'. By this time, the regulations governing the administration of the corporate Communion of the House of Commons at St. Margaret's was developing into a kind of case law. Each member was required to deliver to the appointed supervisors 'a little note of his name and of the place for which hee served . . . immeadyatlye after the receavinge of the wine'. A Member failing to communicate on the appointed day 'shall not, after that day, come into the House, until he shall have received the Communion, in the Presence of some, or One, of the Persons hereafter appointed to that purpose, and the same be certified, and the Certificate thereof be allowed by this House'. In 1628 the Commons started to give directions on how at least some of the money collected at their official services at St. Margaret's was to be disbursed. They instructed the church-wardens that of the forty pounds donated at their communicating and fast in April, twenty pounds should 'be laid out for the poor children of the hospitals; and the other twenty . . . left to the direction of the churchwardens and overseers for the use of the poor of this parish'.

In November 1640 the House of Commons introduced particularly stringent regulations to avoid difficulties arising during the corporate Communion services at which the attendance of all Members was compulsory. These were designed to prevent 'Profanation, and rejection of the Sacrament: and for the securing of this House that no Papist sits here amongst them'. After 1640 and until the end of the Commonwealth, the corporate Communions were discontinued by the House although services with sermons by preachers selected by the House were retained and multiplied. Then on 25 September 1643 Parliament and churchmen gathered together in St. Margaret's to take the Solemn League and Covenant to join with the Scottish Commissioners in swearing with uplifted hands that among other things they would 'extirpate Popery, prelacy, superstition, schism, and profaneness'. Dr John Lightfoot, who as a member of the Westminster Assembly took part in it, has left this eyewitness account of what took place in his diary: 'This morning being met, we had word presently after our sitting into Assembly, that the House of Commons was gone to St. Margaret's Church, and so we went after them. And after a psalm given by Mr Wilson, picking several verses to suit the present occasion, out of several psalms, Mr White prayed near upon an hour. Then he came down out of the pulpit and Mr Nye went up and made an exhortation of another hours long. After he had done, Mr Henderson out of the seat where he sat did the like, and all tended to forward the Covenant. Then Mr Nye, being in the pulpit still, read the Covenant; and at every clause of it, the House of Commons, and we of the Assembly, lift up our hands, and gave our consent thereby to it, and then went all into the Chancel, and subscribed our hands; and afterwards we had a prayer by Dr Gouge, and another psalm by Mr Wilson, and departed into the Assembly again.'

During the Civil War and the Commonwealth period that followed it, parliamentarians expected partisan support from 'their church' but in return accepted their responsibility for contributing towards both its maintenance and its good works. The churchwardens' accounts in 1650 and 1651 bear witness to this, although the church did not always benefit to the full extent of the sums voted by Parliament. The small selection of items from the accounts that follow give some support to these conclusions. There is ample further evidence in the accounts during the following years but the quoted items are reduced to a minimum to avoid tedious repetition.

1650. Item, there was given by the Honourable House of Parliament, for to repair St. Margaret's Church, the summe of two hundred pounds, payable out of Mr Brett's compounding fyne att Goldsmith's Hall; but the same being after transferred to Gurney House, and made payable there out of deans' and chapters' lands, these accomptants, by order of vestry, sould the same to Mr Nicholas Love, at 11/- in the pound . . . 110/-/-.

1651. Item, of the Right Honourable the Council of State, toward reparation and cleaning of the new church yard, after the Scottish prisoners had much annoyed and spoiled the same . . . £30.

Item, paid to the ringers for ringing on the 4th. of September, upon intelligence of the overthrow of the Scottish army at Worcester . . . 6/-.

Item, paid to the ringers for ringing on the 24th. October, being a day of thanksgiving for the victorie over the Scots at Worcester . . . 7/-.

Item, paid for hearbes and lawrell that were strewed in the church the sam day . . . 8/-.

On 23 June 1657, the House of Commons made formal representations to Oliver Cromwell requesting him to 'remove from Margarett's, Westminster, the present Preacher, being a prisoner to the Upper Bench; and also one Warmtree, who is employed as a Lecturer there, being a notorious delinquent; and to appoint some person of eminent godliness and abilities to be public Preacher there'. The result of these representations is recorded in the minutes of St. Margaret's Vestry meetings held on 1 October 1657 and 18 January 1658. At the Vestry meeting in October it was 'Resolved that in obedience to His Highness the Lord Protector's nominacion and appointment bearing date the 22nd of September last and remaining with the Churchwardens, Mr Vyner and Dr Warmstree bee removed from preaching in the Parish Church of Margaret's Westminster and that Mr Edward Pearce bee permitted to preach therein on the Lord's Daie in the forenoones and Mr Seth Wood on the Lord's Daies in the afternoones, and that they the said Mr Pearce and Mr Wood shall have and enjoy such advantages and maintenance as shall bee raised in such sort as hath been usual there.' At the meeting in the following January an amendment was added to the Lord Protector's order with regard to preachers. It was 'that the Churchwardens doe resort unto the several burgesses and assistants of the several wards of this Parish and to consult with them concerning such persons as shall be thought fitt to collect the free benevolence of the inhabitants of this Parish towards the maintenance of the aforesaid ministers.'

Nine years after the Battle of Worcester, a distracted and impoverished England, fearful of a revival of military despotism, summoned the second Charles Stuart to return from exile and take up the reins of government. Charles entered London on 29 May 1660 to the acclaim of the populace and the support of a loyal Parliament offering constitutional support for a Church and State as anti-Catholic as it was anti-Puritan. So at long last, in May 1661, as recorded in the Commons Journals, it was explicitly 'Resolved, upon the Question, That the Sacrament of the Lord's Supper shall, upon Sunday next come Sevennight, being the Twenty-sixth of this Instant May, in the Forenoon, be administered at St. Margaret's Church in Westminster, according to the form prescribed in the Liturgy of the Church of

England; and that all the Members of this House shall then and there receive the said Sacrament; and that whosoever shall not then and there receive the said Sacrament, shall not, after that Day, come into the House, until he shall have received the said Sacrament in the presence of Two or more of the Parties hereafter appointed to that Purpose, and the same be certified, and the Certificate thereof allowed by this House . . . Dr Gunning, and Mr Carpenter, the Chaplain of this House, are desired to officiate at that Time, and to Preach, one of them in the Morning, and the other in the Afternoon.'

However, the traditional order about compulsory participation in the Commons' act of corporate Communion was becoming difficult to enforce. On 30 May, one Member, Andrew Newport, wrote to Sir Richard Leveson: 'There were so many Members absent of both parties from St. Margaret's on Sunday last, when they were appointed to receive the Communion, that neither party thought fit to take notice of it in the House next day. Mr Prynne and some few others refus'd to take it kneeling.' The matter was also noted by Samuel Pepys in his diary in the following terms: 'May 26th. (Lord's Day.) This day the Parliament received the Communion of Dr Gunning at St. Margaret, Westminster. Sir W. Batten told me how Mr Prin (among the two or three that did refuse today to receive the sacrament upon their knees) was offered by a mistake the drinke afterwards; which he did receive, being denied the drinke by Dr Gunning, unless he would take it on his knees; and after that, by another the bread was brought him, and he did take it sitting, which is thought very preposterous.'

It was becoming clear that what the Commons had at first devised as a religious test to exclude Roman Catholics, because their loyalty was suspect was beginning to operate also against Protestant Dissenters. It is certainly significant that whereas in 1666 when certain Members sought the leave of the House to speak against the orders to receive the Sacrament in St. Margaret's, the motion was lost by ninety-eight votes to fifty-four, yet six years later such orders for compulsory corporate Communion ceased to appear in the House of Commons' Journals. It is also indicative of a more tolerant approach to the religious beliefs of Members that in 1672 and again in 1673 Bills promoted to exclude 'Dissenters in matters of religion from the Church of England' from sitting in the House of Commons were defeated on each occasion. Furthermore, the Test Act of 1673 which excluded nonconformists from municipal corporations did not apply to Members of Parliament.

In his book *Church and Parish*, a former rector of St. Margaret's, Charles Smyth, made the following very valid observation: 'To any priest who celebrates the divine mysteries at the altar of the Commons' Church, it must always be a moving thought that in this very chancel the protagonists in the tragic conflict between Crown and Parliament that issued in our Civil War – Wentworth and Pym, Hampden and Falkland, Cromwell and Vane and Hyde – knelt, in a sacred fellowship transcending all personal and public animosities, to receive the most comfortable Sacrament of the Body and Blood of Christ ... Unhappily there was one public animosity which was rather asserted than transcended by this sacred ordinance. The corporate Communion served a dual purpose: not only to unite, but also to exclude. It was not only a corporate Communion: it was at the same time a sacramental test.'

Following the Restoration of the monarchy St. Margaret's continued to fulfil its role as a national church for the use of the House of Commons. When it was in session, the House attended St. Margaret's officially, led by Mr Speaker, upon all such official occasions as the state services on 5 November, 30 January and 29 May, as well as on all general last days and thanskgiving days appointed by Royal Proclamation. As time went on the attendance fluctuated a great deal, but the House continued its established practice of appointing the preachers for their special services, and subsequently to pass a formal motion thanking them and expressing the wish of the House for them to print the text of their sermons. Normally this motion was simply a formality, but not on every occasion. On a fast day appointed by His Majesty's Proclamation, 22 December 1680, Dr Thomas Sprat and Dr Gilbert Burnet preached before the House. The customary vote of thanks was given to Dr Burnet for his sermon, but thanks to Dr Sprat was deliberately withheld. As a result, Dr Sprat, who had become the Minister of St. Margaret's only the year before, was rewarded by the King with a canonry of Windsor!

On 30 January 1700 on the fifty-first anniversary of the execution of the Royal Martyr, a further uncertain element was introduced into the ceremonial religious activities of the Commons in St. Margaret's. The preacher appointed by the House for the occasion was the Revd William Stephens, rector of Sutton in Surrey. In his sermon he asserted that 'the observation of that day was not intended out of any detestation of his murder, but to be a lesson to other kings and rulers, how they ought to behave themselves towards their subjects, lest they should come to the same end'. In the House of Commons on the following day the customary motion of thanks to the preacher was negatived without a division, and it was further resolved: 'That, for the future, no Person be recommended to preach before this House, who is under the Dignity of a Dean in the Church, or hath not taken his Degree of Doctor of Divinity.'

However as the years went by, even a doctorate of Divinity could not guarantee the House against a displeasing sermon. In 1722 the preacher was the Revd Dr Thomas Nowell, Regius Professor of History and Public Orator in the University of Oxford, and Principal of St. Mary Hall. The parliamentary sequel to the sermon (which had taken place during the parliamentary recess) is described in a letter written by Edward Gibbon to his friend Holroyd on 21 February: 'Today the House of Commons was employed in a very odd way. Tommy Townshend moved, that the sermon of Dr Knowell, who preached before the House on 30

January (albeit the House was represented only by the Speaker and four members in St. Margaret's on that occasion) should be burnt by the common hangman, as containing arbitrary, tory, high-flown doctrines. The House was nearly agreeing to this motion, till they recollected that they had already thanked the Preacher for his excellent discourse, and ordered it to be printed. Knowell's bookseller is much obliged to the Right Honourable Tommy Townshend.' Towards the end of this inconclusive debate a Member proposed 'That for the future, the Thanks of this House be not given for any Sermon preached before this House, until such Sermon shall have been printed and delivered at the door of this House.'

The debate was resumed on 25 February with a formal motion to remove from the votes of the House the vote of thanks to Dr Nowell for his sermon, and this was agreed to after debate without a division. The debate, however, seen in perspective bordered on the farcical. The Member who had previously seconded the original vote of thanks to Dr Nowell tried to disclaim responsibility by saying that he had done so against his better judgment but had been over-persuaded by the Member who proposed it. The Speaker explained that he had strongly disapproved of Dr Nowell's sermon, but, having mentioned his disgust to a friend who he was sure would mention his feelings to Dr Nowell, had assumed that Dr Nowell would omit from the printed text the offensive passages. Another Member, Sir Roger Newdigate made an impassioned speech justifying both Dr Nowell and Charles I. Yet another Member, Mr Frederick Montague, observed that 'The clergy of this country are in a very disagreeable situation when they are obliged to preach on the 30th of January. I remember when a clergyman was refused the thanks of the House because he preached in the opposite extreme to Dr Nowell.' He then gave notice that he would introduce a Bill to repeal the statute by which the religious observance of the anniversary was required.

The Bill was debated on 2 March 1772. As was expected, it was opposed by Sir Roger Newdigate. More moderate opposition came from, among others, Mr Stephen Fox who thought it did no harm other than to oblige Mr Speaker to attend church once a year. He also observed that the day was almost forgotten as a fast day, and he certainly never fasted on the day, so he tended to regard the Bill as somewhat irrelevant. The motion to bring in the Bill was lost by 125 votes to 97. However this did not stimulate any increase in the attendance at St. Margaret's in subsequent years on this anniversary. Indeed at the beginning of the nineteenth century Prime Minister Spencer Perceval was distressed to find it 'discreditably thin'.

In spite of the large accommodation reserved at St. Margaret's for the House of Commons, no remuneration in the form of pew rents was ever requested by the church except on a single occasion in 1799 when a mistake was made. This was regarded as such a serious matter that a special meeting of the Vestry was called to correct any misunderstandings that might exist. The meeting was held on 10 April in that year, and the following is an official account of what took place:

'This Vestry was convened for the purpose of enquiring how and under what authority the Right Honourable the Speaker of the Honourable Houses of Commons has been applied to for Rent of Pews in the Church, heretofore and anciently set apart as solely appertaining to him and his attendants.

'Resolved unanimously – That this Vestry never did or could sanction that measure, a measure opposite to the past professions of former Vestries, evidently injurious to the Parish and an illsuited return for the frequent aids granted by Parliament for the Repairs of the Parish Church, and it appearing to this Vestry that such payment originated in the Collectors considering the Speaker as a private Inhabitant upon his first coming to reside in this Parish.

'Resolved also unanimously – That such Payment in future be discontinued.

'Resolved also unanimously – That a copy of these Resolutions signed by the Reverend Dr Fynes as Chairman be sent to the Right Honourable the Speaker, accompanied with the respectful Compliments of this Vestry, and an assurance of their readiness to provide seats in this Church for him and his Attendants in any manner that he may wish.'

In the 1840s the House of Commons appointed a Select Committee on St. Margaret's with a wide ranging brief. The Report of the Committee was published in 1844. It recognised the benefit to

Members of the special accommodation made freely available to the House by St. Margaret's, but was critical of the 'incongruity of this Church in its style of architecture and its close proximity to Westminster Abbey'. It therefore went on to make the unanimous recommendation that the church should be pulled down and removed from its present site to one that would be less populous. The Committee's proposal met with no general approval either from Parliament or from St. Margaret's Vestry and so for the second time in its history, the present building was saved from demolition. Instead of implementing the Committee's recommendation, Parliament voted a grant of £1,200 in 1845 to assist with the cost of necessary maintenance by St. Margaret's to the existing building. This was the penultimate occasion that the House authorised a grant in aid to St. Margaret's and brought the total sum contributed by the House during the eighteenth and nineteenth centuries for the upkeep of its church to £26,570. Members were being made to realise that for Parliament to continue making grants available to one parish church was creating embarrassing precedents in relation to all other parish churches that might be in need of financial assistance for their major works of restoration and maintenance. The next and final official Parliamentary grant was made in 1876 following a meeting in St. Margaret's vestry chaired by Viscount Hatherley and attended by the Speaker of the House of Commons, Mr Brand, who was better known as Viscount Hampden. A motion put to accept the estimates for the cost of removing the galleries and other restoration work was seconded by Mr Speaker, and passed by the meeting. The cost involved was £10,986 towards which the House granted £1,500.

Since that day, therefore, all financial support received by St. Margaret's from Members of Parliament has been on a purely personal basis. In this context it is a matter of record that Members of Parliament have been generous in their response to special appeals, and in their acceptance of responsiblity for the 'Commons' Church'. In 1905, for example, when the east wall was moved and the chancel lengthened as a result by some six feet, the Restoration Committee under the chairmanship of the Rector, Dr Hensley Henson included among its members, Mr Speaker, Sir Michael Hicks-Beach, Mr Asquith, Mr Lyttleton and other MPs who had homes in the small area which formed the ecclesiatical parish at that time. Later in the twentieth century provision was also made for all Members of the Commons, whether resident in the parish or not, to be full members of the church activities. An Authoritative Declaration was made on behalf of the Archbishops of Canterbury and York that for the purposes of the 'Enabling Act' Members of the House of Commons as such have the status, and can exercise the rights of residents in St. Margaret's parish.

Acting on this ruling the rector and senior churchwarden in April 1921 wrote to every Member of the House asking him to enter his name on the Roll of Parochial Electors, and enclosing the usual form of

Declaration. About 200 Members signed. Many of the others were already disqualified because they were enrolled on the parochial rolls of other London churches. The death of the senior churchwarden, Sir Edward Coates, led to some delay in what followed, but in February 1922 a meeting was called of enrolled electors. Nine of the Members present were elected to form a nucleus of a new Parliamentary Church Council with the power to add to their numbers up to a maximum of twenty-five with the condition that the final membership of the Council should be as representative as possible of all the Parties in the House. On 1 May in the same year, the first full Parliamentary Council met in the House of Commons. The meeting unanimously agreed that it would be desirable to inaugurate the opening of each Parliamentary session with an official service in St. Margaret's Church. At a meeting of the Parliamentary Church Council on 27 February 1924 it was resolved that four services should be held in the Crypt Chapel of St. Mary Undercroft in the Palace of Westminster during the period of Lent each year. At a meeting of the Council on 6 December 1928 consideration was given to a request for a memorial tablet to be placed in St. Margaret's in memory of the Rt. Hon. Charles Masterman. The request was strongly supported by twenty-three prominent Members of Parliament including no fewer than fifteen Privy Councillors. The Privy Councillors included such august names as Neville Chamberlain, Winston Churchill, David Lloyd George, Ramsay Macdonald, Walter Runciman, Philip Snowden and

Kingsley Wood. Nevertheless, in spite of the eminence of its supporters, the Council at its meeting agreed that the request for such a memorial tablet should be turned down.

However, ten years later at a Parliamentary Church Council held on 22 November 1938 it was resolved, 'That a tablet, whose design the Council had inspected and approved, should be erected by Members of the House of Commons in memory of the late Canon Carnegie, Rector of Saint Margaret's and Chaplain to the Speaker of the House of Commons.' The Second World War decimated St. Margaret's lay organisations, and so far as the Parliamentary Church Council was concerned the position was further exacerbated during the immediate post war years by the substantial changes that took place in the composition of the House both as regards political Parties and individual membership. Inevitably the first ten years after the war were largely taken up with the tasks involved in trying to restore the physical damage sustained by the building and the revival of the church's basic role as a parish church.

Eventually, a general meeting took place in a committee room of the House of Commons at which it was decided to form a Parochial Church Council to consist of the surviving members of the former Parliamentary Church Council with the addition of six non-parliamentary members to be elected by resident parishioners in accordance with the Representation of the Laity 1956 Act. The declared intention expressed at the meeting was to achieve the aim of moving towards a Parochial Church Council that would consist ultimately of the Speaker, the rector, two churchwardens, six Members or officers of the House of Commons, and six other members elected by persons on the electoral roll of the church. The whole object of the proposal was to retain the close association with the House of Commons, but at the same time to give regular Sunday members of the congregation a voice in the affairs of the church. The decision of the general meeting was put into effect on 30 May 1963, and the Parochial Church Council continued in existence until St. Margaret's ceased to have a parish in 1973. Without a parish there could of course be nothing 'parochial' about its Council which, during the years that followed, gradually evolved into a St. Margaret's Committee with fewer members.

However, since 1973 there has been no weakening of the close links that bind St. Margaret's to the House of Commons. Since the 1972 Act which became effective in 1973 there has been a warden appointed from the Members of Parliament serving on the Committee. In addition all the rectors of St. Margaret's since that date have also been chaplains to the Speaker in an unbroken line. Furthermore there is a legal obligation in the 1972 Act to maintain all the rights of Members of Parliament in relation to St. Margaret's that existed before the passing of the Act. Under the miscellaneous provisions of the Act, Clause 19 states that 'Nothing in this Act shall affect the customary rights of the Members or officers of either House of Parliament in relation to St.

Margaret's Church or Westminster Abbey.' Westminster Abbey is included in the clause since it is the
official church of the House of Lords.

Due to their commitment to their constituencies
throughout the country, very few Members are able
to attend Sunday services in St. Margaret's, and
those who do attend when they are in London, can
do so only infrequently. In spite of this the church is
filled with Members and staff of the House of
Commons on a number of occasions throughout
each year when special services are held on week-
days. Every year on Tuesday early in December at
6.00 p.m. a Parliamentary Carol Service is held in St.
Margaret's for the House of Commons and the staff
of Westminster Hospital. Following a nineteenth
century precedent, the collection is donated to
Westminster Hospital. The one hour service en-
compasses nine hymns and carols, and lessons read
by both Parliamentarians and members of the
hospital staff. It always finishes promptly at 7.00
p.m. to enable MPs to return to the House in time for
any votes that may occur at that time. Every year
also sees a number of memorial services in memory
of former Members of the House of Commons.
These services are arranged outside the time of the
sitting of the House, and for them the church is
always well filled with Members and staff wishing to
pay their tributes to a late colleague.

House and church are also united at other kinds of
special service, like the one held on each occasion of
the Opening of Parliament. On the actual day of the
State Opening of Parliament the bells of St.

Margaret's ring out their hymn of praise and thanksgiving. Sometimes the church may be the scene of an historic Parliamentary event which is mainly attended by the regular Sunday congregation that is largely non-parliamentary. On Sunday, 3 March 1991 the Rt. Hon. Bernard Weatherill, MP became the first Speaker of the House of Commons ever to preach a sermon from the pulpit of St. Margaret's on the occasion of a regular prayer book service since it became the Commons' Church in 1614. For the benefit of Members who were in their consituencies, or otherwise unable to attend on that Sunday morning, the sermon was broadcast on BBC Radio 4. Mr Speaker took as his text The Book of Proverbs 29: 18; 'Where there is no vision the people perish'. He was speaking shortly after the end of the Gulf war.

In one of the very telling passages in his sermon he observed that, 'We have too many men of science; too few men of God. We have grasped the mystery of the atom and rejected the Sermon on the Mount. Man is stumbling through a spirtual darkness while toying with the secrets of life and death. The world has achieved brilliance without wisdom, power without conscience. Ours is a world of nuclear giants and ethical infants.' He spoke of the need to get the balance right between material progress and spiritual value, and he drew his sermon to its close by saying: 'Perhaps it is not without significance that the House of Commons continues today in the rebuilt Chapel of St. Stephen, and that daily before we proceed to the "cut and thrust" of the debate, the

150

Chaplain to the Speaker – the present Rector of St. Margaret's – leads the House in prayer.'

The prayers spoken by the rector of St. Margaret's at the beginning of each sitting day in the Chamber of the House of Commons constitute one of the strongest links in the chain that continues to bind the Commons to its special church. It is appropriate, therefore, that this chapter should conclude with one of those prayers which has a special significance for each Member present in the debating chamber at the start of the day's parliamentary session:

Almighty God, by whom alone Kings reign and Princes decree justice; and from whom alone cometh all counsel, wisdom and understanding; We thine unworthy servants, here gathered together in thy Name, do most humbly beseech Thee to send down thy Heavenly Wisdom from above, to direct and guide us in all our consultations: And grant that, we having thy fear always before our eyes, and laying aside all private interests, prejudices and partial affections, the result of all our counsels may be to the glory of thy blessed Name, the maintenance of true Religion and Justice, the safety, honour and happiness of the Queen, the public wealth, peace, and tranquility of the Realm, and the uniting and knitting together of the hearts of all persons and estates within the same, in true Christian Love and Charity one towards another, through Jesus Christ our Lord and Saviour.

AMEN

Return to the Abbey

The analogy of the family is eminently appropriate to describe the origins of, and explain the relationship between, the church of St. Margaret of Antioch and the Abbey at Westminster established to honour St. Peter. Both were ordered to be built by King Edward the Confessor between the years 1051 and 1064. Building work on the Abbey began in 1051 and it is believed that the first monks moved into the completed domestic quarters in 1061. They included ten monks transferred from Exeter who were very familiar with the details of the martyrdom of St. Margaret. In *c.* 1064, as the Abbey church neared completion, King Edward ordered the building of an adjacent parish church to augment the spiritual activities of the monks by providing facilities for corporate worship and pastoral care for the residents of Westminster. In deciding on the Patron Saint for the new church, King Edward was undoubtedly advised by the ten monks who had been transferred to Westminster from Exeter three years earlier. Thus, from the very beginning, St. Margaret's became a sister church to the Abbey, and the Abbey, according to H.F. Westlake, assumed the responsibilities of the rector of St. Margaret's and received the tithes of the parish.

The earliest administrative document referring to St. Margaret's which is still on the record shows that Abbot Herbert, who died in 1140, made a grant of sixty shillings from the profits of the parish church towards the service of the High Altar and the needs of the entire Church of Westminster. The first time an attempt was made to drive a wedge between church and monastery was in the second half of the twelfth century, when Gilbert Folliot claimed jurisdiction over St. Margaret's. The resolution of this dispute between bishop and abbot was effected by the Papal Bull of 1189 which confirmed that the church was firmly under the rule of the Abbot of Westminster and outside the area of responsibility of the Bishop of London. Pressure for the transfer of St. Margaret's to the Diocese of London continued for another thirty years until the famous Papal Decree of 1222 defined the precise area over which the Abbot of Westminster excercised full authority with total exemption from episcopal rule. The Decree is quoted in full in the Abbey Domesday Book as well as in the history of the Abbey by Flete – a fifteenth century monk. Within the jurisdiction of the Abbey was included 'the Church of St. Margaret with its whole parish, with all the chapels contained within the said parish, with their tithes and all their appurtenances'.

The close family relationship that continued to exist between church and monastery until the Reformation, did not greatly inhibit St. Margaret's from exercising a considerable degree of independence in managing its own affairs. The major rebuilding of St. Margaret's that took place between 1487 and 1523 contrasted vividly with the desultory interest in the new work on the Abbey throughout its slow progress from the middle of the fourteenth century onwards. The cost of rebuilding St. Margaret's was unequally divided between the monks of the Abbey who, as Rector, financed only the completion of the choir, and the parish which initiated the work and paid for the new nave and the aisles in their entirety. The order in which the work was carried out to avoid disruption of the services as much as possible, and the distribution of the costs indicate clearly that the dominant partner was the church. Thus although the family connection continued, the younger sister was becoming increasingly independent.

The first real break between the monastery and the church occurred on 16 January 1540 when Abbot William Boston effectively signed away his rectorial rights to St. Margaret's by appending his name to the deed surrendering the monastery to Henry VIII. Prompt action by the churchwardens in petitioning the King enabled them to obtain possession of all rights to the revenue from the payments for graves, which had been the main source of regular income formerly paid to the monastery. This severance of the financial link between the two continued until August 1542 when the former Abbot Boston was installed as the Dean of the Abbey and Collegiate Church of St. Peter, and was thus able to reclaim his rectorial rights and the fees pertaining to them. St. Margaret's has always been somewhat reluctant to follow fashion and the changes required to implement the Reformation of the English Church were effected at a slower pace than in the Abbey. When the removal of tabernacles and other furniture and fittings was eventually carried out, these were, whenever possible, purchased by churchwardens and other influential members of the church to be preserved against the day when they might again be installed.

During the years that followed, feelings ran high about the extent and the nature of the reforms and there is evidence in the churchwardens' accounts of St. Margaret's that at times the parishioners were less than disciplined in expressing their feelings when utterances from the pulpit did not accord with their own precisely held views. In the accounts for 1548–50 it is recorded that eighteen pence was 'payd to William Curlewe for mendynge of dyvers pewes that were brokyn when Dr Lattymer dyd preache'. Underlying the somewhat primitive, if violent, demonstrations of religious fervour was the developing and more profound conflict between Parliament and Puritanism on the one hand and the prerogative of the Sovereign and Prelacy on the other. The events of 1614, when the House of Commons effectively showed its preference for St. Margaret's as its chosen place of worship, resulted

155

from a widening of the gulf between the Puritanism of the church and the Prelacy of the Abbey. The subsequent association between Commons and church ensured the continued devotion of St. Margaret's to the Book of Common Prayer and to the new and growing brand of Puritanism that prevailed until the Restoration. Whilst this at no time threatened to sever the family ties with the Abbey of St. Peter, it was the source of a number of family quarrels, and occasionally led to the House of Commons attempting to usurp the prerogatives of the Abbey in relation to St. Margaret's with varying degrees of success until the time of the Restoration.

In 1640, Stephen Marshall who was known to have expressed his antipathy to Charles I with unpardonable rudeness was appointed to preach before the House of Commons in St. Margaret's on two occasions. At this time the Curate and Lecturer appointed by the Dean and Chapter of the Abbey was a Dr Gilbert Wymberley. The minutes of the Vestry meeting on 27 February 1641 recorded the choice of Stephen Marshall 'to be theire lecturer being recommended to them by the Honoble. House of Commons to take his place ye next Lord's Day after ye feast of the Annunciacon next ensueing. This selection was made in the presence of Dr Wymberley the present lecturer of the said Parish who voluntarily resigned his place and consented to the choice of Mr. Marshall.' The story is continued in the Journals of the House of Commons. The Journal dated 25 October 1643 shows that the House 'Ordered that Mr Recorder, Mr Wheeler, and

Mr Bell do take some course that St. Margaret's Westminster may be furnished with godly Preachers on the Lord's Day in the Afternoon.' This was followed by an order in the Journal dated 29 November '. . . that Mr Recorder, and Mr Wheeler do bring in an ordinance for sequestring the Profits of the Vicarage of St. Margaret's, Westminster, and the Tythes belonging unto it, to make provision for an able Minister to preach there.'

The House of Commons administered the final *coup de grâce* to the Abbey's choice of curate on 12 February 1644 when it voted in favour of 'An Order for sequestring of the Rents and Profits of the Curateship of the Parish Church of St. Margaret, Westminster, whereof Dr Wymberley is now Curate, to the use of Samuel Gibson, B.D., a learned and orthodox Divine, who is hereby appointed and required to preach every Lord's Day there, and to take care for the discharge of the Cure of that place, in all the duties thereof, and shall have be due to His Majesty out of the said Church, the Vicarage House, together with all Tythes, Oblations, Emoluments, Fees, Stipends and Profits whatsoever, belonging to the said Vicarage, or to the Curateship of the said Church, until further Order shall be taken by this House.' However, so long as the Dean and Chapter retained, if only in name, the office of Rector of St. Margaret's, the family link remained unbroken.

After the Restoration of the monarchy the functions and responsibilities of the Rector of St. Margaret's once again resided firmly in the hands of the Dean and Chapter of the Abbey. The Dean then took the opportunity to right some of the wrongs that had arisen from the bigoted actions of Parliament in relation to the church during the Commonwealth period. However the independence of the churchwardens in the day-to-day administration of the church and parish remained firmly based on a wholly democratically based system of annual elections. The system is very fully described in the Vestry minutes of 17 April 1679 as follows:

'The Church Wardens are chosen according to ancient custom of the said Parish, time out of mind, the Thursday before Whitsunday after the manner following:

'There is a Bell appointed to be tolled, by which the Parishioners have notice, and thereupon doe repayre unto the Church to see the Church Wardens, which be going out of their office, deliver up their accompt and ballance-moneys, and also to understand who be Church Wardens for the year ensuyng.

'Then they have a table sett in the Chancell, at which the Doctor or Minister of the Parish, and the rest of the Vestrymen do sit, and thither the Church Wardens in being bring their accompts fairly engrossed and bound up in vellum, together with the balance-moneys. The ancient Vestrymen at the upper end of table receiving the same, and inspecting at least the totall summes of what hath beene received, what paid, and what remains to adjust the Church Wardens' accompt.

'Then they order and appoint some that have already executed the same office of Church Wardens to auditt their accompts, and within one month do make report thereof unto them. This being done, the Vestrymen adjourn from thence into the Vestry Room, and there take out of the records the names of former Overseers of the Poor the names of eight or ten persons, and set them down in this manner, A.B., C.D., always setting down the younger of the present Church Wardens first, and then they debate the fittest man for that office; and so everyone crossing those whom they judge the meetest for it, they that have the most crosses have it.' There is an air of familiarity about the process.

Some twelve years earlier there had been an attempt at sharp practice when a minority of those eligible to vote attempted to replace with their own selections two properly elected wardens. After the minister and most of the vestrymen had left the church, two disappointed candidates, Mr Baker and Mr Edwards, persuaded a few remaining vestrymen to elect them to be churchwardens. In consequence of their claim a trial was held before the judge of the official court of the Dean and Chapter. The judge, the Rt Worshipful T. Exton made his judgment in favour of the real churchwardens, and this judgment was upheld on appeal to the King's Majesty and a Court of Delegates consisting of the Bishops of Wincester and Rochester, the Lord Chief Justice, a Mr Justice Twisden, and three Doctors of Law.

From the beginning of the eighteenth century new difficulties between church and Abbey began to manifest themselves. These were the outward signs of a quarrel that had its roots in the seventeenth century during the period of the Parliamentary Commonwealth. At that time the affairs of the Dean and Chapter had been largely administered by a 'Committee of the College of Westminster' under the chairmanship of Sir Robert Pye. Sir Robert Pye was a parishioner of St. Margaret's and its most prominent vestryman during that period. It is not altogether surprising that when executive power was returned to the Dean and Chapter at the time of the Restoration there should be a residue of ill will existing between the Abbey and St. Margaret's Vestry. Suspicion and resentment continued between them well into the nineteenth century and the period was punctuated by a series of disputes. In July 1713 came the abortive attempt by the Dean to appoint a new parish clerk of St. Margaret's. This was followed later in the year by a dispute about the right of the Abbey to the fees which were received for funerals at St. Margaret's.

It began when one of the prebendaries from the Abbey and the Receiver made an examination of the burial registers in September 1713. Four months later the Dean and Chapter proceeded to assert their rights to the funeral fees being paid to St. Margaret's. Since the establishment of the Commonwealth such fees had been paid by the sexton to the church-wardens who had retained them on behalf of St. Margaret's. An order was then sent to the sexton ordering him henceforward to pay the fees to the Abbey Receiver. He agreed to do this in the future, but explained that all past payments were in the hands of the churchwardens. The Abbey then ordered that a 'Bill of Discovery' he brought against the churchwardens for an account of the fees they had received. This was ignored and so two months later a further Bill was brought requiring an account of fees received in regard to funerals and burials in St. Margaret's churchyard, and demanding to know the nature of the churchwardens' title to them. The records do not show whether either 'Bill of Discovery' was ever successful, but they do show that the animosity between Abbey and church did not lessen in the ensuing years.

After Dean Atterbury was committed to the Tower it was thought that more amicable relations might develop. Two years after the event, in 1725, a petition from St. Margaret's churchwardens and overseers to the Dean and Chapter for help towards the relief of the poor of the parish received a gracious and practical response. Then in 1728 the Dean consecrated St. Margaret's new daughter church 'The new chapell at Millbank' now known as St. John's Church, Smith Square, and St. Margaret's was responsible for the appointment of the vestrymen. However a new dispute arose in 1737 arising from the claim of the Dean and Chapter to total jurisdiction over Tothill Fields in the parish of St. Margaret. In that year the Dean and Chapter forbade the inhabitants to hold fairs on Tothill Fields. This was resisted on the ground that Letters Patent granted by Henry III and other subsequent Royal Licences had granted the right to a weekly market on Mondays and an annual three-day fair to be held there over the feast of St. Mary Magdalene.

This dispute was resolved in favour of the Dean and Chapter. In May 1754 St. Margaret's Vestry served notices on the Prebendaries to appear before the vestrymen to show cause why they should not pay the rate assessed upon their houses. A careful search of the Abbey records was on this occasion sufficient to provide adequate precedents in support of the Abbey.

The acquisition and installation of St. Margaret's beautiful Renaissance East Window in 1758 was the cause of a much more serious dispute between the Abbey and the church. A minute in the Chapter Book dated December 1758 records that it was 'Ordered That Doctor Bettesworth our Commissary be directed to make an enquiry concerning the painted Figures in the East-Window and other new Ornaments, placed lately in The Church of St. Margarett without any Faculty granted for the same: and that the Treasurer do from time to time pay such expenses as shall be necessarily occasion'd by such enquiry.' The prosecution was instituted in the name of Daniel Gell, the Registrar in the Ecclesiastical Court of the Dean and Chapter. Mr Gell was also a vestryman of St. Margaret's and his involvement on behalf of the Abbey produced a prompt response from St. Margaret's as recorded in the following Vestry minute: 'Feb. 8, 1759. That Daniel Gell Esq. be struck off the List of Vestrymen of this Parish and that the Clerk do not summon him to any further Vestry.' The objection of the Dean and Chapter was that the East Window contained superstitious images, particularly as it represented the Crucifixion, in contravention of an Act passed in the reign of Edward VI for 'abolishing and putting away divers Books and Images'. The case was stoutly defended by St. Margaret's churchwardens and dragged on for more than three years.

The Curate of St. Margaret's at this time was Dr Thomas Wilson who was also a Prebendary of the Abbey, and who dissented from the order for the enquiry. In 1761, whilst the case was still in progress, Dr Wilson's book *The Ornaments of Churches considered* was published. This was written about the case and achieved wide acclaim. For his efforts he received the unanimous thanks of the Vestry, and copies of his book were ordered to be sent to the Earl of Bath and to the two Members of Parliament for Westminster. There is no doubt that the book played a major role in determining the outcome of the issue, and in May 1762 Mr Gell notified the churchwardens that it was not intended to proceed further with the case. The Dean and Chapter proposed that the Vestry should pay the costs of the action but in return the Dean would undertake not to recommence the suit. At the meeting of the Vestry, the proposal was unanimously rejected, and the churchwardens resolved that in the future they would move against the Abbey for costs if any fresh suit were begun. There the matter rested.

In 1763 one of the two named churchwardens in the case, Mr Samuel Peirson, presented a handsome and richly chased cup, stand, and cover to the overseers of the parish in commemoration of the successful conclusion of the vexatious suit brought against his colleague and himself. The silver gilt cup, stand and cover together weighed 93.15 ounces. The cup bore the figure of St. Margaret and the stand bore the arms of Peirson. Samuel Peirson's popularity with his fellow vestrymen was clear from a Vestry minute dated 4 December 1761. This records that Mr Churchwarden Peirson applied for leave to erect a monument in the church to his own memory, and this was unanimously granted to him free of any of the fees which were customarily paid for the erection of monuments.

Tothill Fields were again the subject of a dispute in 1806. The Dean and Chapter had erected a house there, but this had been demolished by 'Some person or persons pretending to act under the authority of the parish of St. Margaret Westminster'. Then in 1831 another cause of contention arose over the control of St. Margaret's churchyard, when the Dean and Chapter vetoed an attempt by the churchwardens to erect stands there from which to view the coronation procession of William IV. On this occasion the authority of the Dean and Chapter in its role of Rector of St. Margaret's was upheld.

In 1835 the Tory reformer, Sir Robert Peel, created the Ecclestiastical Commission to reform the medieval administrative system, or lack of system, of the Established Church. In 1840 an Act was passed by Parliament to carry into effect, with certain modifications, the Fourth Report of the Commissioners of Ecclesiastical Duties and Revenue. This was a substantial piece of legislation embracing ninety-four clauses which dealt comprehensively with the organisation and the revenues of Bishopricks, Cathedrals, Collegiate Churches, and Ecclesiastical Corporations. Clause 1 of the Act stipulated that 'from henceforth all the Members of Chapter, except the Dean, in every Cathedral and Collegiate Church in England, and in the Cathedral Churches of St. David and Llandaff, shall be styled Canons . . .' Clauses 29, 30 and 31 dealt specifically with the relationships between St. Margaret's, the Collegiate Church of St. Peter, and the Diocese of London, and the future arrangements for a canon to be rector of St. Margaret's in place of the Dean and Chapter. Thus for the first time in its history, St. Margaret's was wholly independent of the Abbey in name as well as in fact.

The relevant part of Clause 29 of the historic Act of 1840 reads as follows: 'And be it enacted that the Rectory of the Parish of Saint Margaret in the City of Westminster shall immediately and be permanently annexed and united to the Canonry in the said Collegiate Church of St. Peter, Westminster, held by Henry Hart Milman, Clerk, Master of Arts . . . and the said Henry Hart Milman and his successors, shall as Canons of the said Church, become *ipso facto* Rectors of the said Parish and the said Parish Church thereof, to all Intents and Purposes; and the said Parish shall become Part of the Province of Canterbury, of the Diocese of London, and of the Archdeaconry of Middlesex; and the said Parish and the Rector, and other Ministers and Officers thereof shall, in Ecclesiastical Matters, be subject only to the Jurisdiction of the

Archbishop of Canterbury, the Bishop of London, and the Archdeacon of Middlesex . . . and be exempted and relieved from all other Ecclesiastical Jurisdiction whatsoever; Provided always, that nothing herein contained shall in any Manner affect or prejudice any of the Rights, Customs, or Claims of the Parishioners of the said Parish of Saint Margaret, or the Vestry or Churchwardens thereof for the Time being . . .'

Clause 30 of the Act transfers a house from the Dean and Chapter to provide accommodation for the rector of St. Margaret's. By the standards of legislative clauses it is concise and unequivocal. It says: 'And be it enacted, That such One of the Prebendal Houses belonging to the Chapter of the Collegiate Church of Saint Peter, Westminster as shall be determined on by the Authority herein-after provided, shall be, as soon as conveniently may be, exempted from the Rule of Option subsisting in the Chapter thereof, and be permanently annexed to the said Canonry now held by the said Henry Hart Milman, and shall thenceforth be the House of Residence for the Rector of the said Parish of Saint Margaret for the Time being.'

Clause 31 deals with the division and application of the finances applicable to the canon as a member of the Chapter, and as rector of St. Margaret's. It also makes provision for the stipends and accommodation for the ministers appointed to the Broadway Chapel (a daughter church) in the parish of St. Margaret.

Thus, for the first time in the 776 years of its

history, the Abbey no longer had any jurisdiction over St. Margaret's. The Dean and Chapter agreed with the terms of the Act. Whether this was due to a loss of patience with St. Margaret's over the many disputes which had arisen during the previous years, or whether it was a recognition of the benefits accruing to the Established Church from the reforming zeal of Sir Robert Peel is not clear. The fact remains that for the next 133 years St. Margaret's remained outside the jurisdiction of the Dean and Chapter of the Abbey. It ordered its affairs and managed its finances as independently as any other parish church within the Diocese, and for nearly a hundred years it prospered. Not only was the parish in central Westminster big enough and wealthy enough to sustain it, but a succession of brilliant and often controversial rectors attracted a strong following from outside the parish and even as far afield as the United States of America. Towards the end of the nineteenth century the fame and the beauty of the church grew with the acquisition of new treasures paid for in dollars as well as in pounds sterling. In the twentieth century, its site and reputation sustained it as a national and a fashionable church.

However, changes in the parish boundary as, over the centuries, daughter churches acquired their own parishes, and population changes in the twentieth century parish of St. Margaret combined to create a threat to the continued independence, if not the survival, of the church. Residential accommodation in a large area at the centre of the parish had given place to government and Parliamentary offices, as well as large blocks of commercial premises. The substantial reduction in the number of residents gave rise to serious concern by the middle of the century. Wide ranging consultations took place between the government and church authorities to seek a solution to the growing problem. It was finally agreed to divest St. Margaret's of its parochial duties and return it to the Abbey Close. With the agreement of the Archbishop of Canterbury, the Bishop of London, and the Dean and Chapter of Westminster Abbey, and to the relief of those who continued to worship at St. Margaret's, legislation to that end was introduced and received the Royal Assent on 27 July 1972. This was the Westminster Abbey and Saint Margaret Westminster Act 1972. It came into operation on 1 June 1973.

The purpose of the Act was 'to provide for the division for ecclesiastical purposes between Westminster Abbey and the adjoining parishes of the parish of Saint Margaret, Westminster, and for the dissolution of that parish and its Rectory; to provide for the vesting in the Dean and Chapter of Westminster of the church of Saint Margaret Westminster and certain other property held for its benefit and for the maintenance by the Dean and Chapter of that church and the services to be held therein; and for other services'. Therefore, legislative provision was made for the division of the parish into three parts. The central part which consisted of St. Margaret's Church, St. Margaret's Churchyard, and the Royal Palace of Westminster was to be removed from the Province of Canterbury, the Diocese and Archdeaconry of London, and the Rural Deanery of Westminster, and added to the Close of Westminster Abbey with the Dean as the Ordinary subject only to the jurdisdiction of Her Majesty as Visitor. The remaining two parts of St. Margaret's parish were added to the parishes of St. Martin-in-the-Fields, Westminster, and St. Matthew's, Westminster.

Under the Act the Dean and Chapter have responsibility for the appointment of one of their number to be in charge of St. Margaret's Church. Authority is also given for the minister in charge of St. Margaret's to be styled the rector for the purpose of style and designation but not for any other purpose. The church, churchyard and all other property previously belonging to the church are now vested in the Dean and Chapter, but provision has been made in the Act to preserve a degree of independence in the day-to-day activities of St. Margaret's. For example, Clause 13 subsection (2) states that 'For the purposes of the registration of baptisms and marriages solemnised in St. Margaret's Church, St. Margaret's Church shall be treated as if it had remained the parish church of a separate parish . . .' The relationship with the House of Commons which has endured since 1614 is also safeguarded in Part IV of the Act under the miscellaneous provisions.

Clause 18 states that 'Nothing in this Act shall affect the status of, or any jurisdiction over, the Chapel of Saint Mary Undercroft (commonly known as the Crypt Chapel of the Palace of Westminster)'; and Clause 19 states quite unequivocally that 'Nothing in this Act shall affect the customary rights of the members or officers of either House of Parliament in relation to Saint Margaret's Church or Westminster Abbey.' A further clause, Clause 21, also safeguards the rights in respect of baptism, marriage and the holding of a funeral service in St. Margaret's Church of all those who were resident in the parish immediately before the Act came into force and who were on the church electoral roll.

So it is that St. Margaret's has returned to the Abbey family. As in all families, the relationship that exists between the church and the Abbey depends to a great extent on the personalities and attitudes of the people directly involved. Happily during the twenty years since the Act was passed there has developed a close understanding and warmth of affection between those who serve St. Margaret's and those who serve the Abbey church of St. Peter. On the occasions when joint functions are held there is a genuine 'family' atmosphere and a strongly felt community interest as each complements the work of the other. This close, relaxed relationship has been facilitated by the substantial change in the nature of St. Margaret's that was brought about by the 1972 Act. For the first time since it was established in 1064, St. Margaret's is no longer a parish church and no conflict of interest can arise in relation to the church between the Dean and Chapter and the Diocesan authorities. Furthermore, all the previous experience of a family relationship between the two churches from 1064 until 1840 had been based on the authority of the Abbot and later the Dean and Chapter, acting as rector and appointing the curate of St. Margaret's. At the same time, particularly during the period from the fifteenth to the eighteenth centuries, the elected churchwardens and the Vestry, conscious of their responsibilities to the parish, became increasingly powerful and increasingly resentful of interference in anything they regarded as their proper function.

With such possible causes of confrontation now eliminated, a happy association has developed within which the Dean and Chapter provide St. Margaret's with the administrative and financial services back up it needs as a Royal Peculiar and House of Commons' Church. In return St. Margaret's is able to extend the scope of the Abbey Close with alternative and complementary facilities to those available from the Abbey. This is not entirely dissimilar from the respective roles of an eleventh century monastery and the church built nearby to augment its work for the community. Although with the passing of the centuries the activities and responsibilities of each have undergone change, the relationship between the church of St. Margaret and the Collegiate church of St. Peter has returned in the twentieth century to the principle of the relationship that was established in the eleventh century between church and monastery. It would seem to be a formula that works, and it augurs well for the future of both churches.

Appendix A

Officiating Clergy appointed to St. Margaret's

Undated	Simon, *Chaplain*
	Robert, *Chaplain*
	Alexander, *Chaplain*
1316	Thomas de Cherlecote, *Chaplain*
1366	William, *Chaplain*
1366	Ralph, *Chaplain*
1388	William, *Sacerdos*
1416	John Latener, *Chaplain*
1466	Richard Saxilby, *Chaplain*
1484	William Kempston, *Chaplain*
1497	Sir William Morowe, *'Masse Priest'*
1503	Sir John Conyers, *Curate*
1509	Sir John Symes, *Curate*
1519	James Hall, *Curate*
1521	Sir Robert Danby, *Curate*
1524	Sir Henry Mote, *Curate*
1530	William Tenant, *Curate*
1540	Sir Henry Mote, *Curate*
1552	Sir Olyver Lyngard, *Curate*
1562	Sir Thomas Sowdeley, *Curate*
1564	Humfry ffletcher, *Curate*
1566	Sir Robert Danyell, *Curate*
1572	Edmund Taw, *Curate*
1575	James Johnson, *Curate*
1576	George Row, *Minister*
1580	William Holonde, *Curate*
1584	George Dickeridge, *Minister*
1586	Edmond Medowcroft, *Minister*
1590	Richard Burton, *Minister*
1592	Francis Kay, *Minister*

1594	William Draper, *Curate*
1598	Richard Bentley, *Curate*
1602	William Murrey, *Curate*
1621	Sir Prosper Styles, *Curate*
1622	Sir Isaac Bargrave, *Minister*
1628	Vincent Peirce, *Curate*
1637	Dr Gilbert Wymberley, *Minister*
1640	Stephen Marshall, *Lecturer*
1642	Samuel Gibson, B.D. (*Appointed by Parliament*)
1644	Mr Eaton, *Minister*
1647	John Binns, (*Elected by the Vestry*)
1652	Mr Garrett, *Minister*
1657	Mr Vyner, *Preacher*
1661	Dr William Tucker, *Curate*
1664	Dr William Outram, *Curate*
1679	Dr Thomas Sprat, *Curate*
1683	Dr Nicholas Onley, *Curate*
1720	John Herbert, *Minister*
1724	Dr Edward Gee, *Curate*
1730	Dr Scawen Kenrick, *Curate*
1753	Dr Thomas Wilson, *Curate*
1784	Dr John Taylor, *Curate*
1788	Dr Charles Wake, *Curate*
1796	Dr Charles Fynes, *Curate*
1828	James Webber, *Curate*
1835	Henry Hart Milman, M.A. (*Curate 1835–40*) (*Rector 1840–49*)
1849	Dr William Cureton, *Rector*
1864	William Conway, M.A., *Rector*
1876	Dr Frederic William Farrar, *Rector*
1895	Robert Eyton, M.A., *Rector*
1899	Dr Joseph Armitage Robinson, *Rector*
1900	Dr Herbert Hensley Henson, *Rector*
1913	William Hartley Carnegie, M.A., *Rector*
1936	Vernon Faithfull Storr, M.A., *Rector*
1941	Dr Alan Campbell Don, *Rector*
1946	Charles Hugh Egerton Smyth, M.A., *Rector*
1957	Michael Staffurth Stancliffe, M.A., *Rector*
1970	David Lawrence Edwards, M.A., *Rector*
1978	John Austin Baker, M.A., *Rector*
1982	Trevor Randall Beeson, M.A., *Rector*
1987	Dr Donald Clifford Gray, *Rector*

Appendix B

Memorial Windows Destroyed in the Second World War

In memory of **Lady Arabella Stuart**, designed by Clayton and Bell and executed by H.G.A. Halliday.

In memory of the **Trollope Family**, designed and executed by Clayton and Bell.

In memory of **Lord Hatherley**, the Lord Chancellor from 1868 to 1872, designed and executed by Clayton and Bell.

In memory of **Lady Hatherley**, designed and executed by Clayton and Bell.

In memory of **Anne Wainwright**, designed and executed by Clayton and Bell.

In memory of **Lord Farnborough**, formerly **Sir Thomas Erskine May**, Clerk of the House of Commons, designed and executed by Clayton and Bell.

In memory of the **Jubilee of Queen Victoria**, designed and executed by Clayton and Bell.

In memory of **Sir H.A. Hunt**, designed and executed by Edward Frampton.

In memory of **Edward Lloyd**, Master Printer, designed and executed by Edward Frampton.

In memory of **Sir Goldsworthy Gurney**, Engineer and Inventor, designed and executed by Edward Frampton.

Note: All the clear glass windows in the clerestory above the nave were also severely damaged by high explosive.

174

Appendix C

The 10 bells of St. Margaret's Church, Westminster

The 4 Treble bells, No 6 and the Tenor recast and the ring of ten re-hung with new fittings in the old oak framework strengthened by Gillett & Johnston of Croydon, 1939

NO	NOTE	INSCRIPTIONS	WEIGHT		
			Cwt	Qr	Lb
1	F#	Lester & Pack of London Fecit 1761			
		Recast by Gillett & Johnston, 1939	5	2	8
2	E	All as No 1	5	3	26
3	D	S*K*1739			
		Recast by Gillett & Johnston, 1939	6	2	8
4	C#	All as No 3	6	3	18
5	B	S*K*1739	7	3	24
6	A	Robert Catlin Fecit 1739			
		Recast by Gillett & Johnston, 1939	9	1	9
7	G	Robert Catlin Fecit 1739	11	1	13
8	F#	Mr Thos. Hatch & George Stubbs Esqr			
		Church Wardens 1773			
		T. Janaway Fecit	12	0	27
9	E	Thomas Mears of London Founders 1834			
		James Webber D.D,			
		Minister St Margaret's			
		William Forty & Robert Bryan,			
		Churchwardens	14	1	19
10	D	Dr Thos. Wilson, Minister			
		Saml. Peirson & Wm. Ielfe,			
		Churchwardens 1761			
		Lester & Pack of London Fecit			
		Recast by Gillett & Johnston, 1939	26	0	26

Bibliography

Carpenter, Edward and **Gentleman**, David, *Westminster Abbey* (1987)

Carrington, R., *Westminster City School and its Origins* (1983)

Edwards, David L., *St. Margaret's Westminster* (1973)

Gray, Donald, *Chaplain to Mr Speaker* (1991)

Hellinga, Lotte, *Caxton in Focus* (1982)

Rosser, Gervase, *Medieval Westminister, 1200–1540* (1989)

Sinclair, Mrs. J.E., *History and Description of the Windows of the Parish Church of the House of Commons* (1906)

Smyth, Charles, *Church and Parish* (1955)

Walcott, Mackenzie, *The History of the Parish Church of St. Margaret in Westminster; from its foundation in AD 1064* (1847)

Westlake, H.F., *St Margaret's Westminster* (1914)
Westminster, A Historical Sketch (1919)

Index

Index

178